12 MONTHS OF FUN!

THE LOBSTER KIDS' GUIDE
TO EXPLORING
SAN DIEGO

BY DINA JO MADRUGA

Lobster Press™

Madruga, Dina Jo, 1964-
The Lobster Kids' Guide to Exploring San Diego
Text copyright © 2002 Lobster Press™
Illustrations copyright © 2002 Lobster Press™

Published by Lobster Press™
1620 Sherbrooke Street West, Suites C & D
Montréal, Québec H3H 1C9
Tel. (514) 904-1100, Fax (514) 904-1101
www.lobsterpress.com

Publisher: Alison Fripp
Editor: Alison Fischer
Copy Editor: Frances Purslow
Cover Illustration: Christine Battuz
Icons: Christiane Beauregard and Josée Masse
Layout and Design: Zack Taylor

Distribution:
In the United States   In Canada
Advanced Global Distribution Services   Raincoast Books
5880 Oberlin Drive, Suite 400   9050 Shaughnessy Street
San Diego, CA 92121   Vancouver, BC V6P 6E5
Tel. (858) 457-2500   Tel. (800) 663-5714
Fax (858) 812-6476   Fax (800) 565-3770

We acknowledge the financial support of the Government of Canada
through the Book Publishing Industry and Development Program
(BPIDP) for our publishing activities.

National Library of Canada Cataloguing in Publication Data

Madruga, Dina Jo, 1964-
    The Lobster kids' guide to exploring San Diego

(Lobster kids' city explorer series)
Includes index.
ISBN 1-894222-52-0

    1. Family recreation—California—San Diego—Guidebooks.
2. Children—Travel—California—San Diego—Guidebooks.
3. Amusements—California—San Diego—Guidebooks.
4. San Diego (Calif.)—Guidebooks. I. Fischer, Alison, 1977- II. Title.
III. Series.

F869.S22M37 2002   917.94'9850454   C2001-903850-X

Printed and bound in Canada

Table of Contents

Author's Introduction   7
A Word from the Publisher   9
The Lobster Rating System   11
Table of Icons   12

Chapter 1 · Local Attractions   13
Introduction   14
Balboa Park   15
Coronado   17
Gaslamp Quarter   19
Legoland, Carlsbad   21
Old Town   23
SeaWorld   25
Wild Animal Park, Escondido   27
World-Famous San Diego Zoo   29

Chapter 2 · In Your Neighborhood   31
Introduction   32
Bookstores and Other Retailers   33
Bowling Alleys   34
Children's Libraries   36
Costumes and Party Supplies   37
Crafty Places   38
Farmers' Markets   40
Ice and Roller Rinks   41
Places to Paint Pottery   43
Recreation Centers   44
Skateboard Parks   45
Swimming Pools and Surf Lessons   46

Chapter 3 · Places to Play   **49**
Introduction   50
Belmont Park   51
Family Beaches   52
Family Fun Centers   53
Indoor Gyms   55
Indoor Rock Climbing   56
Knott's Soak City, Chula Vista   57
Seaport Village   59
Ultrazone   60
Other Places to Play   62

Chapter 4 · Places to Learn   **63**
Introduction   64
Birch Aquarium at Scripps, La Jolla   65
Children's Discovery Museum, Carlsbad   67
Museum of Making Music   69
Museum of Man   71
Reuben H. Fleet Science Center   73
San Diego Model Railroad Museum   75
San Diego Museum of Art   77
San Diego Natural History Museum   79
Other Places to Learn   81

Chapter 5 · Music, Theater, Dance & Cinema   **85**
Introduction   86
California Center for the Arts, Escondido   87
CCT and CYT, El Cajon   88
Fern Street Circus   90
Old Globe Theatre   91
San Diego City Ballet   93
San Diego Junior Theatre   94
San Diego Symphony   96
Special Cinema   98
Starlight Theatre   100
Other Music, Theater, Dance & Cinema   101

Chapter 6 · Animals, Farms and Zoos   103
Introduction   104
Bell Gardens, Valley Center   105
Children's Pool, La Jolla   106
Chula Vista Nature Center, Chula Vista   108
Free Flight Aviary, Del Mar   110
Helen Woodward Animal Center, Rancho Santa Fe   111
Places to Pick Fresh Produce   113
Places to Ride   114
Tidepools   115
Other Animals, Farms and Zoos   116

Chapter 7 · Green Spaces   117
Introduction   118
Lake Poway, Poway   119
Los Penasquitos Canyon Preserve   121
Mission Bay Park   122
Mission Trails Regional Park   124
Presidio Park   126
Quail Botanical Gardens, Encinitas   127
Tijuana River Estuary, Imperial Beach   129
Torrey Pines State Reserve, La Jolla   130
Other Green Spaces   132

Chapter 8 · Historical Sites   135
Introduction   136
Cabrillo National Monument   137
Chinese Historical Museum   139
Firehouse Museum   141
Maritime Museum   142
Mission San Diego de Alcala   144
Old Poway Park, Poway   146
San Pasqual Battlefield State Park, Escondido   148
Villa Montezuma   149
Other Historical Sites   151

Chapter 9 · Getting There is Half the Fun   153
Introduction   154
Amtrak Trains   155
Bicycle and Pedicab Tours   156
Boat Tours and Other Aquatic Adventures   158
Bus and Trolley Tours   160
Cinderella Carriage Company   162
San Diego Trolley   163
Sky Rides   165

Chapter 10 · Favorite Festivals   167
Introduction   168
Carlsbad Flower Fields, Carlsbad   169
Christmas on the Prado   170
Fleet Week   172
Lakeside Western Days and Rodeo, Lakeside   173
Ocean Beach Kite Festival   174
Oktoberfest, La Mesa   176
San Diego County Fair, Del Mar   177
U.S. Open Sandcastle Competition,
  Imperial Beach   179

Room & Board:
  Kid-friendly Restaurants   181
  Family-friendly Hotels   184
12 Months of Fun! Directory of Events   187
Index   191

Author's Introduction

What a treat, to write about my sun-baked corner of the States, where my kids grow up traipsing the halls of historic missions, collecting shells along the bubbly Pacific and conquering tree-lined mountain trails. My family regularly thrills to the whims of world-class theme parks, yet finds nature—filled with tidepools and flower fields—as compelling as anything contrived. In the same day, we can sit among thousands and cheer for Shamu, then in solitude applaud the sunset from the cliffs at Torrey Pines. Until I had children, I couldn't find anyone who loved exploring like I did. But now I'm gifted with two joyous explorers who've helped uncover our hometown's many wonders—and they're all documented in this book. So let the sun sit on your shoulder, hold tight to a little hand and come exploring!

This book is dedicated to Mom and Dad for their positive spirit, sense of humor, and love of reading and writing—attributes that have influenced me well; to my kids Kaley and Ryder, who taught me it's okay to love life and treasure this time; and my husband Pete, who encourages all my endeavors—no matter where they lead.

A special thanks to May Nasser and the gang at San Diego Automotive Museum for granting me time to write this book, and my *San Diego Family Magazine* friends, Sharon Bay and Claire Fadden, for their enduring support. And of course, thanks to Alison Fischer and the Lobster Press staff who gave me the chance to write this book and share my favorite San Diego adventures with so many others.

DINA JO MADRUGA

A Word from the Publisher

In 1998, Lobster Press™ published its first book, *The Lobster Kids' Guide to Exploring Montréal*. Since then, the Kids' City Explorer Series has grown and now includes 13 guides to other major Canadian and American cities.

Whether you're a tourist or resident, parent or teacher, this book is a complete resource of things to do and see with kids in the San Diego area. It's jam-packed with valuable, time-saving information and great ideas for outings.

The sites in this guide were visited by Dina Jo Madruga and her family in 2001 and the information given has been verified. However, since prices and business hours are subject to change, call ahead to avoid disappointment. Please accept our apologies in advance for any inconveniences you may encounter.

To get the most out of this guide, please familiarize yourself with our "Lobster Rating System" and table of icons. These features let you know what our author's family thought of each site and what amenities are available. Also, please note that traveling distances to the sites were determined from Old Town.

If you have comments about this book, please visit our website and complete our on-line survey. Let us know if we've missed your family's favorite destination and we'll include it in the next edition!

A last word: Please be careful when you and your children visit the sites in this guide. Neither Lobster Press nor the author can be held responsible for any accidents that might occur.

Enjoy! And watch for the other books in the Kids' City Explorer Series, now available: Boston, Chicago, Las Vegas, New Orleans, San Francisco and Seattle.

FROM THE GANG AT LOBSTER PRESS™

The Lobster Rating System

We thought it would be helpful if you knew what Dina Jo Madruga and her family thought about the sites in this book before you head off to visit them. They rated every attraction and activity they visited for its:

☞ enjoyment level for children
☞ learning opportunities for children
☞ accessibility from Old Town
☞ costs and value for the money

A one-lobster rating: Good attraction.

A two-lobster rating: Very good attraction.

A three-lobster rating: Excellent attraction.

Not fitting some of the criteria, and subsequently not rated, are green spaces and various similar, nearby or other attractions.

Table of Icons

These facilities and/or activities are represented by the following icons:

Beach		Picnic tables		
Bicycling		Playground		
Birthday party		Restaurant		
Bus stop		Restroom		
First aid		Swimming		
Hiking		Telephone		
Ice cream stand		Trolley		
In-line skating		Wheelchair/ stroller accessible		
Information center		Wildlife watching		
Parking				

Automobiles are certainly the most popular mode of getting around Southern California, and San Diego is no different. Many visiting families choose to rent a car, secure a map and navigate area freeways to the destinations in this book. But don't overlook public transit options. The San Diego trolley zips about to handy depots throughout the county. Metropolitan Transit Service (MTS) buses can always get you where you want to go. All public transit directions in this book originate from Old Town Transit Center and stops are less than a ¼ mile walk from your destination. For more information on public transit, visit www.sdcommute.com or call (800)COMMUTE. See Chapter 9 for details.

CHAPTER 1

LOCAL ATTRACTIONS

Introduction

San Diego is one of the most popular family destinations on the planet—little wonder since it is home to such big-time attractions as SeaWorld and the World-Famous San Diego Zoo. Aside from these two well-known wonders, San Diego harbors many other family-friendly adventures and serves up everything you could dream of in a Southern California vacation—including lots of laughs and a bit of learning as well.

From historic Old Town, a trip to the Zoo is only minutes away. You'll find the rare beauty and cultural celebration of Balboa Park nearby, home to museums and gardens. A short jaunt across a blue bridge carries families to Coronado—a beautiful city and an attraction all its own, teeming with parks, beaches, historical sites, shopping and dining. Less than an hour north, experience exotic animals amidst a safari adventure at the Wild Animal Park, or visit Legoland, the newest and most "constructive" member of the local theme parks. Of course, Shamu and friends provide a splashing good time at Sea-World, and the Gaslamp Quarter is another destination waiting to be discovered in delightful San Diego.

Rare Beauty
BALBOA PARK

1549 El Prado, San Diego
(619) 239-0512
www.balboapark.org

Swathed in swaying palms and striking architecture, Balboa Park is home to 15 museums, an array of gardens (from the formal English variety to a stark desert collection), performing arts venues, children's rides and other recreational and cultural institutions.

Stroll the Prado to the Visitor Center, where informative staff share Balboa Park secrets. Along the way, enjoy the ornate Spanish Colonial buildings originally constructed for the 1915 Southern California Exposition. Hear bells chime from the 198-foot California Tower while you decide which museums to visit. Be it sports, history, automotive, science, natural history or the Model Railroad Museum (page 75), there's an interest for all.

Take a free ranger-led tour of the park, enjoy street performers, visit the Botanical Building, or relax in grand style at the Organ Pavilion and enjoy a free concert every Sunday at 2 pm. Also on summer Sundays, the International Cottages open their doors for a trip "around the world," including authentic food and lawn programs. Families flock to performances at the Marie Hitchcock Puppet Theatre (held Wednesday through Sunday). The Junior Theatre, Old Globe and Starlight (page 100) are also located on site. On the north side of the park by the zoo, kids can ride the miniature train, the hand-carved carousel from 1910 and the butterfly ride for $1.25 each.

Fancy some exercise? Find hiking and biking trails to the east, or visit Morley Field's golf course, Velodrome, swimming pool, tennis courts and more. The complimentary Balboa Park Tram makes getting around this 1200-acre cultural haven a snap.

SEASONS AND TIMES
➤ Year-round: Daily, 10 am–4 pm. Kiddie rides: Summer (mid-June–Labor Day): Daily, 11 am–5 pm. Winter (Labor Day–mid-June): 11 am–5 pm, weekends and holidays only. Alternating museums are free each Tuesday of the month. Call for details.

COST
➤ Free.

GETTING THERE
➤ By car, travel on Hwy. 163 south to Park Blvd. Turn north and follow the signs. Enter at President's Way, Space Theatre Way or Village Place. From Interstate 5 south, take Pershing Dr., then follow Florida Dr. west. Follow Zoo Place west to Park Blvd. Turn south and proceed to Village Place, Space Theater Way or President's Way. Free parking on-site. About 10 minutes from Old Town.
➤ By public transit, take bus route 7/7A/7B to stop at Park Blvd. and Village Place. Head west into the park.
➤ By bike, follow the car directions from Park Blvd., or take Sixth Ave. and enter at Laurel St.

NEARBY
➤ Coronado, San Diego Zoo, Gaslamp Quarter, Chinese Historical Museum, Villa Montezuma.

COMMENT
➤ Plan a 4-hour visit.

Urban Oasis
CORONADO

**1047 B Ave., Coronado
(619) 437-8788
www.coronadovisitors.com**

C oronado floats upon the ocean, connected
to the mainland only by a thin isthmus and
Coronado Bay Bridge, a two-mile expanse
that transports visitors to a beautiful oasis only
minutes from the city. Coronado is known as the
"Crown Village" and is dotted with Victorian
homes, stately mansions, abundant parks, public
tennis courts, multi-use trails, sandy beaches and
a golf course. For a glimpse into San Diego's glam-
orous past, stop in at Hotel del Coronado and view
the towers and turrets, then head inside for a self-
guided walking tour through the Hall of History.

A best bet for families is Tidelands Park, with its
playground, fitness course, ball fields, grassy lawns
and a small tranquil beach near the base of the
Bridge. The paved trails aren't crowded, making
biking and in-line skating along the shore easy for
young children. Interpretive signs offer interesting
tidbits about waterfowl and other features. The route
leads to Ferry Landing Marketplace that's filled with
shops and dining, as well as Ferry Landing, where
bikes and people travel across the bay aboard the
San Diego Coronado Ferry.

Orange Avenue is lined with shops, restaurants,
and bike and skate rentals. The Glorietta Bay Inn

offers a walking tour of Coronado and their marina rents watercraft (619-435-3101). If you're looking for culture try the Coronado Playhouse, Lamb's Theatre or the Coronado Historical Museum. Stop in and take a Navy Base Tour for an appreciation of San Diego's naval history. Camp on the beach at Silver Strand State Beach. Up for the unusual? Loew's Resort hosts gondola cruises (page 158).

SEASONS AND TIMES
➤ Year-round: Daily. Contact the Visitors Bureau for specific information on individual sites.

COST
➤ Free.

GETTING THERE
➤ By car, travel Interstate 5 south to Hwy. 75/Coronado Bridge. (Toll is $1, car pools free). About 15 minutes from Old Town.
➤ By public transit, board ferry at 1050 N. Harbor Dr. or at the Coronado Ferry Landing (619-234-4111).

NEARBY
➤ Seaport Village, Gaslamp Quarter, Balboa Park, San Diego Zoo, Maritime Museum, Chinese Historical Museum, Villa Montezuma.

COMMENT
➤ Plan at least a 4-hour visit.

Hip & Happening
GASLAMP QUARTER

**Bordered by 4th Ave., 6th Ave.,
Broadway and Harbor Dr., San Diego
(619) 233-5227
www.gaslamp.org**

The Gaslamp Quarter spans 16 blocks and is filled with restaurants, eclectic shops, galleries and theaters housed in historic Victorian buildings. To learn the area's history, the Heath Davis House (619-233-4692) offers a two-hour guided walking tour on Saturdays at 11 am. It is a bit lengthy for younger children so if you prefer, pick up a walking map for $2 and strike out on your own.

Stop by the Old Gaslamp Ice Cream Company at 503-5th Ave. for a sweet treat. If you're feeling active, head to Gaslamp Bicycle and Pedicab where you can rent bikes or take a pedicab ride (page 156). The nearby Martin Luther King Promenade provides a relaxing retreat with open play space and fountains that your kids will enjoy. Playfully designed Horton Plaza shopping center dominates the northern side of Gaslamp and is teeming with tyke-tempting retailers, including FAO Schwartz and the Disney Store.

See a flick at the Horton Plaza Theatre, or at the nearby state-of-the-art Pacific Gaslamp 15 Cinema. The surrounding restaurants serve up every type of cuisine imaginable, from Irish to Japanese to

Italian. Visit either the International Visitor Information Center at 11 Horton Plaza (619-236-1212) or at Sixth & L St. (619-232-8583) with questions you may have.

If you want to experience a bit of New Orleans at night, this is a great place to do it. Once the sun sets, the Gaslamp Quarter is transformed into an urban festival with music seeping out of the various clubs, and the streets and sidewalks jam-packed with people dressed up and ready to party.

SEASONS AND TIMES
➤ Year-round: Daily. Individual activity hours vary. Call for details.

COST
➤ Free.

GETTING THERE
➤ By car, take Interstate 5 south to Front St. and follow it to Broadway. Turn east, then south on Fourth Ave. Street parking is metered and difficult. Try validated parking in the Horton Plaza parking structure at Fourth Ave. and F St. About 10 minutes from Old Town.
➤ By public transit, take bus route 5A and get off at Market St. and 6th Ave. Walk north into the Gaslamp. Or ride the trolley (Blue Line) and exit at Gaslamp Quarter Station.

NEARBY
➤ Balboa Park, Coronado, Firehouse Museum, Seaport Village, San Diego Zoo, Maritime Museum, Chinese Historical Museum, Villa Montezuma.

COMMENT
➤ Plan a 4-hour visit. No wheelchairs/strollers access in Heath Davis house.

Brick by Brick
LEGOLAND

I Lego Dr., Carlsbad
(877) LEGOLAND
www.legoland.com

Yes...believe it! Those tiny, brightly colored building blocks have inspired an entire theme park. Step into the surreal feel of Legoland, where 30 million Lego™ bricks have been used to create some surprising structures. Look closely at everything—it's likely to be made of Legos™!

Most rides throughout the park are tame—a tad too tame for most kids over eight. Your youngest will love to cruise her own car at Driving School, or captain a ship at Skipper School. The Dragon Coaster, perched on Castle Hill, coasts merrily through Legoland Castle and provides a thrill for youngsters, while across the way "steeds" carry riders on the cute and clever Royal Joust.

Older children and adults appreciate the Spellbreaker (a suspended coaster) and the Lego™ Technic Coaster (both have some speed and sharp curves). Miniland USA is also a hit, where landmarks such as the White House, Mount Rushmore and San Francisco's Chinatown are carefully reproduced at a ¹/₂₀th scale. The Imagination Zone offers creative, hands-on possibilities for young and old including Maniac Challenge (complete with computers and Lego™ software). Build & Test is a car-creation station, and Mindstorms is for building and programming robots. Duplo™ Play is the most fun for tots.

The Amazing Maze and the Sky Cycle (demanding pedal power for a view of the park) are enjoyable for the whole family. Cool down at Waterworks, a play area complete with spouting fountains designed to get you wet. The Lego™ Factory tour is worthwhile and there are a few interesting shows to round out the day. FunTown Market offers fresh food if you've got a hungry bunch. It is handily located next to the Family Care Center, which has bottle warmers, rockers, high chairs and diaper-changing facilities. Legoland also offers day camps and birthday parties.

SEASONS AND TIMES
⇥ Year-round: Daily, 10 am—5 pm. Hours extended in summer.

COST
⇥ Adults $38, children (3 to 16) $32, under 3 free.

GETTING THERE
⇥ By car, take Interstate 5 north to Cannon Rd. Exit east and go to Legoland Dr. Turn south and follow signs. About 45 minutes from Old Town.
⇥ By public transit, take the Coaster to Poinsettia Station and take bus route 344.

NEARBY
⇥ Carlsbad Flower Fields, Museum of Making Music, Children's Discovery Museum of North County.

COMMENT
⇥ Plan to spend the day. Diaper-changing areas in all restrooms. Lockers available.

Start at the Beginning
OLD TOWN

San Diego Ave. and Twiggs St., San Diego
(619) 220-5422
www.oldtownsd.com

Stroll back in time among the historic buildings, museums, exhibits, grassy expanses
and gorgeous native plants of Old Town—
considered the birthplace of California. Little red
Mason Street School, circa 1865, still has primers
on the shelves, tiny desks in straight rows and a
dunce cap ready for the unruly. La Casa de
Estudillo, an original adobe home, charms children with its authentically furnished rooms, inviting courtyard and small garden.

For more interactive fun, meet a gunslinger or a
schoolmarm at Seeley Stable, where guided
"evening lantern" tours by docents in period dress
depart nightly. (There are daytime tours too. Stop by
the Visitor Center for more information.) Seeley
Stable displays cowboy saddles and other trappings,
but be sure to peek around back to find carriages,
covered wagons and the blacksmith shop.

Looking for a not-too-spooky thrill? Head to
Whaley House, where knowledgeable volunteers tell
the history of this haunted house and its ghosts. Visit
the graveyard where some of San Diego's earliest
inhabitants are buried—even Yankee Jim, a con-
victed horse thief! Dining options (from snack bars
to fine fare) are abundant in Old Town, but the patio

at Casa de Bandini is probably the most kid-comfy, with umbrella-shaded tables amid blooming foliage, babbling fountains and strolling mariachis.

SEASONS AND TIMES
➤ Old Town: Year-round, daily. Visitor Center: Year-round, daily, 10 am–5 pm.

COST
➤ Old Town Historic State Park: Free. Whaley House: Adults $4, children (5 to 17) $2, under 5 free.

GETTING THERE
➤ By car, from Interstate 5 take the Old Town Ave. Exit and travel east. Turn north on San Diego Ave. (becomes Congress St.) From Interstate 8, take the Taylor St. Exit and travel west. Turn east on Juan St. Parking is free but difficult to find.
➤ By public transit, ride the Blue Line trolley and disembark at the Old Town Transit Center. Walk east into Old Town.
➤ By bike or on foot, follow Sports Arena Blvd. or SeaWorld Dr. to Pacific Hwy. Go west at Taylor St. Proceed past Trolley Station (bike racks available).

NEARBY
➤ Presidio Park, SolidRock Gym.

COMMENT
➤ Plan a 4-hour visit. Arrive early (especially on weekends). Whaley House closed Tuesdays.

Rapids, Pirates and Sharks, Oh My!
SEAWORLD

SeaWorld Dr., San Diego
(619) 226-3901
www.seaworld.com

This San Diego landmark has undergone exciting changes in recent years, adding such attractions as Wild Arctic, Shipwreck Rapids and Pirates 4-D. With incredible aquariums, hands-on exhibits, clever play areas and fabulous shows, SeaWorld is the epitome of "edutainment."

At Rocky Point Preserve, kids can feed the dolphins while at the California Tide Pool, they can hold a starfish or sea urchin. Get chilly at Penguin Encounter or go underwater (via glass tunnel) to grin at toothy sharks in the Shark Encounter exhibit. At Shamu's Happy Harbor, active tykes can romp around the two-acre play area with cargo nets for climbing, colorful ships for clambering and fountains to play in. Bring along a change of clothes so your kids can splash without worry.

If it's a hot day, cool off in the "Splash Zone" during the Shamu show, or board Shipwreck Rapids for an unforgettable whitewater ride. Pirates 4-D is a humorous 3-D movie with an added physical dimension, including water blasts, gusts of air and simulated bird poop. Most kids over six love the excitement, but younger kids may find it over-whelming. At Wild Arctic, a simulated helicopter ride offers the chance to meet walruses, polar bears and beluga whales. Experience a snow shower and sneak through a slumbering polar bear's cave.

Younger children enjoy the cuddly costumed characters found throughout the park, while bigger kids like the Coco Locos Arcade. The Skytower and Skytram provide an elevated view of the surroundings. Seemingly "fish out of water," a pair of Clydesdales reside at SeaWorld and offer opportunities for grooming, hitching and other equestrian care. The SeaWorld Education Department offers teacher materials, camp programs and birthday parties. Annual passes and group discounts available.

SEASONS AND TIMES
➤ Summer: Daily, 9 am—11 pm. Winter: Daily, 10 am—6 pm. Subject to change, call for confirmation.

COST
➤ Adults $41.95, children (3 to 11) $31.95, under 3 free.

GETTING THERE
➤ By car, from Interstate 5, take SeaWorld Dr. Exit and head west following the signs. From Interstate 8 west, exit at West Mission Bay Dr. and follow the signs. About 15 minutes from Old Town.
➤ By public transit, take bus route 9 to SeaWorld stop.
➤ By bike or on foot, travel along SeaWorld Dr. or West Mission Bay Dr. to entrance.

NEARBY
➤ Belmont Park, Mission Bay Park.

COMMENT
➤ Plan to spend the day. Stroller rentals, lockers and diaper-changing facilities available.

A *Quick Trip to the Serengeti*
WILD ANIMAL PARK

15500 San Pasqual Valley Rd., Escondido
(760) 747-8702
www.wildanimalpark.org

Don your hiking boots and a wide-brimmed hat for this unique adventure that tempts you to imagine you're crossing the Asian and African plains to see herds of rhino, zebra, antelope and other species—all living naturally. It can get hot, dusty and downright exhausting exploring this 1,800-acre wildlife preserve, but where else can you giggle while an Australian lorikeet sits on your shoulder, or hand-feed a majestic Baringo giraffe? Your children will love ogling the 2,000 animals that call this park home.

The Wgasa Bush Line electric monorail whisks passengers along a 50-minute ride across the simulated plains of the Serengeti and beyond to view exotic and endangered creatures (sit on the right-hand side to get the best view). At the Heart of Africa, take an easy hike through an interactive research island. Pause for a breather at the Samburu Jungle Gym, where kids love to swing like monkeys and parents can relax at shaded picnic tables. Near Mombasa Lagoon, kids will find the opportunity to skip across giant, floating lily pads or hide out in an aardvark's den.

Education and the preservation of endangered species is the mission of the Park and is evident throughout the facility—from the informative interpretive signs and interactive possibilities throughout the park, to the merchandise sold in the gift shops. The Wild Animal Park boasts several unique programs including photo caravan tours and "Roar and Snore" campovers. Annual passes, San Diego Zoo combo tickets, and group discounts are available. The Park sits in an interior valley, so be sure to cover the kids with plenty of sunscreen and carry extra drinking water in summer.

SEASONS AND TIMES
➤ Year-round: Daily, 9 am with varied closing times. Call for current hours.

COST
➤ Adults $25.45, children (3 to 11) $18.45, under 3 free.

NEARBY
➤ California Center for the Arts, San Pasqual Battlefield State Park.

GETTING THERE
➤ By car, from Hwy.163 heading north, proceed to Interstate 15, then to the Via Rancho Parkway Exit. Head east and follow the signs. About 40 minutes from Old Town.

COMMENT
➤ Plan to spend the day. Rental strollers, motorized wheelchairs, binoculars and camcorders available.

Animals Galore
WORLD-FAMOUS SAN DIEGO ZOO

🐝 🐝 🐝

**2920 Zoo Dr., San Diego
(619) 234-3153
www.sandiegozoo.org**

This incredible compilation of flora and fauna truly deserves its lofty moniker. Over 3,800 animals live in this astoundingly natural landscape (including over 6,000 rare species of vegetation) crafted to include caves, rocks, water-falls and swinging jungle vines.

When you arrive, stop to meet the flamingos just beyond the front gate. The zoo encompasses 100-square miles of hilly, trek-able terrain, so take a few minutes to plan your adventure and make use of the moving sidewalks located handily throughout the park. If you'd rather not walk, a 35-minute double-decker bus tour is available for an overview of the zoo, and Kangaroo Bus Tours provides "hop on, hop off" service all day long.

On foot, descend Tiger River where you'll meet crocodiles, pythons and tigers that frequently gaze eye-to-eye with spellbound youngsters. Visit Ituri Forest for an underwater appreciation of hippos, and Polar Bear Plunge for a peek at inhabitants of the Arctic tundra. Gorilla Tropics is another exceptional spot, as is the Rainforest Aviary where brilliant birds come close and tropical showers are typical.

Breezing overhead, the Skyfari Skytram provides a bird's eye view of the park. Of course, the Children's Zoo offers up-close-and-personal encounters with many furry friends.

In the summer, Nighttime Zoo has extended hours with magicians, music and more. The zoo also maintains an exceptional educational department offering various programs (619-557-3969). Annual passes and combo tickets (with admission to the Wild Animal Park), as well as group discounts are available. Self-guided audio tours are offered in five languages.

SEASONS AND TIMES
➤ Summer (mid-June—early Sept): Daily, 7:30 am—9 pm. Winter (early-Sept—mid-June): Daily, 9 am—4 pm.

COST
➤ Daily, adults $19.50, children (3 to 11) $9.50, under 3 free.

GETTING THERE
➤ By car, travel Interstate 5 south to Pershing Dr. Turn west at Florida St. and proceed to Zoo Place. From Interstate 8, take Hwy. 163 south and exit at Park Blvd. Go north and continue to Zoo Place, turn west. Free parking on-site. About 10 minutes from Old Town.
➤ By public transit, take bus route 7/7A/7B to stop at Park Blvd. and Zoo Place.
➤ By bike or on foot, take A St. east to 12th Ave./Park Blvd. Head north and follow car directions. Bike racks south of main entrance.

NEARBY
➤ Balboa Park, Coronado, Gaslamp Quarter, Chinese Historical Museum, Villa Montezuma.

COMMENT
➤ Plan to spend the day. Diaper-changing facilities in most restrooms. Locker, stroller and wheelchair rentals available.

CHAPTER 2

IN YOUR NEIGHBORHOOD

Introduction

Family fun often sprouts up in your own back-yard. Look in your own neighborhood for playful, enriching destinations—many of which are inexpensive or free. Local libraries offer a treasure trove of books and videos, and also provide storytelling, homework help, crafts and other programs. Farmers' Markets are an opportunity for outdoor shopping with an old-time feel, and often include clowns and face painting. Seek out the recreation centers, crafty places, skateboard parks and other friendly little niches for easy entertainment throughout San Diego—sometimes the best sites are right under your nose.

The following chapter invites you to discover the many possibilities in your area and the neighbor-hoods beyond. You'll find a few specific suggestions to get you started and resource numbers for more information. For additional suggestions of family fun in San Diego, visit www.signonsandiego.com and follow the Entertainment or Sports and Recreation link.

Be a Bookworm
BOOKSTORES AND OTHER RETAILERS

Now more than ever, children are encouraged to be bookworms. Retailers such as Barnes & Noble and Borders have made book shopping a kid-friendly experience, maintaining a large selection of books in every possible area of interest. Families are invited to curl up in comfy chairs amidst the rows of hard-covers, paperbacks, videos and CDs. The restrooms are easily accessible and if your brood is peckish, there's often a café where you can munch on tasty treats. The children's areas offer scaled-down furniture, colorful rugs and such terrific programs as reading clubs and story times. Kids can even meet beloved literary characters and authors of their favorite books. Most sites listed below have additional locations, so when inquiring about the children's programs, ask for a store near you.

Retailers such as Zany Brainy and Learning Express are kid-smart too. In addition to selling toys that teach, they offer free kids' events and activities. Visit their websites for store locations, easy science projects, activity calendars and information on summer reading clubs.

BARNES & NOBLE
7610 Hazard Center Dr., San Diego
(619) 220-0175

BORDERS BOOKS AND MUSIC
159 Fletcher Pkwy., El Cajon
(619) 593-5119

BOOKSTAR
3150 Rosecrans Place, San Diego
(619) 225-0465

LEARNING EXPRESS
10755 Scripps Poway Pkwy., San Diego
(858) 695-7888

ZANY BRAINY
5475 Grossmont Center Dr., La Mesa
(619) 466-6751

No More Gutter Balls
BOWLING ALLEYS

Kids find it difficult to keep the bowling ball out of the gutter. But at the establishments listed below, bumper bowling eliminates gutter balls altogether so your kids knock over pins every time.

A great hot or rainy day activity, bowling alleys also offer video games and other on-site amusements. Some alleys even serve up kid-favorites such as cosmic bowling or galactic bowling (a disco-like atmosphere with light shows). Smoking is no longer allowed, so bowling alleys have become much cleaner. Most offer birthday parties and youth leagues, as well as theme sessions and seasonal programs.

Call to check for family activities before heading out—then prepare to don funky shoes and roll out the fun. Check your yellow pages for additional bowling centers or contact the San Diego Bowling Association (619-275-7322).

BRUNSWICK PREMIER LANES

845 Lazo Court, Chula Vista
(619) 421-4801
Video screens, light shows, cosmic bowling, birthday parties, bumper bowling and youth leagues.

GROVE BOWLING CENTER

6348 College Grove Way, San Diego
(619) 287-7000
A 60-lane site with galactic bowling, birthday parties, bumper bowling and youth leagues.

MIRA MESA LANES

8210 Mira Mesa Blvd., San Diego
(858) 578-0500
Birthday parties, bumper bowling and youth leagues.

PARKWAY BOWL

1280 Fletcher Pkwy., El Cajon
(619) 448-4111
Birthday parties, bumper bowling and youth leagues. Adjacent to Boardwalk (page 62).

SUNSET BOWL

3093 Clairemont Dr., San Diego
(619) 276-2240
Birthday parties, "xtreme bowling" and youth leagues.

Cozy Nooks
CHILDREN'S LIBRARIES

There are two library systems operating in San Diego County—the San Diego Public Library and the Serra Cooperative Library System. Between them, they reach thousands of families by providing books, CDs, videos, filtered Internet access, homework help, storytelling, crafts and summer programs (including varied entertainment and reading incentive rewards).

Children enjoy the "grown-up" privilege of owning their very first library card—and a chance for them to begin learning responsibility. First cards are free, but there's a small charge for replacements. Videos generally require adult checkout.

For complete listings of library locations, check your phone book in the government pages. Visit www.sannet.gov/public-library/ for city library locations or www.serralib.org for county library locations to obtain complete service information.

SAN DIEGO PUBLIC LIBRARY
Children's Room at the Central Library
820 E St., San Diego
(619) 236-5838
Offers information on the 33 branch libraries, as well as story times and other special services.

SERRA COOPERATIVE LIBRARY SYSTEM
5555 Overland Ave., Bldg. 15, San Diego
(858) 694-2414
Call for information regarding branch libraries, which stretch into north and south San Diego counties, East County and Imperial Valley.

Party On!
COSTUMES AND PARTY SUPPLIES

One of the most wonderful parts of child-hood is being able to make-believe—mas-querading as a pirate, fairy princess or police officer. The following sampling of sites facilitates a trip to fantasyland, enticing tykes with props, masks, make-up and more.

How about a Hawaiian-themed sleepover for a dozen little girls? Find flowery artificial leis, hula skirts and a pineapple piñata at Party City, which stocks everything you'll need for any party. In addi-tion to the aisles of invitations, plastic tableware, décor, balloons, candy and novelties, it's stocked year-round with adult and children's costumes. There may be a Party City location near you (call or visit their website).

Professional costume suppliers such as Gypsy Treasure and Buffalo Breath Costume Company accommodate kids too, with complete costume sales, rentals and a large selection of accessories. Check the yellow pages for additional places under Costumes or Party Favors, Supplies and Services.

BUFFALO BREATH COSTUME COMPANY
2050 Hancock St., San Diego
(619) 297-1175
Rents and sells theatrical-quality costumes, stocks wigs, boas, masks and make-up.

GYPSY TREASURE COSTUMES
8127 La Mesa Blvd., La Mesa
(619) 466-2251
Costumes for rent or sale, a full line of clown supplies, varied
accessories and discounts for school and church groups.

PARTY CITY
8330 Rio San Diego Dr., San Diego
(619) 295-4200
www.partycity.com
Complete party supplies, as well as costumes and accessories.
Locations county-wide.

Beautifully Busy
CRAFTY PLACES

At neighborhood crafty places, young and old have an opportunity to get creative, artistic and deliciously messy. From large chain stores to tiny craft shops, most establishments offer classes and workshops, supplies and plenty of ideas.

Art Tours in La Jolla provides everything from studio fine art instruction to outdoor art adventure. Knorr Candle Shop and the Basic Bear Factory serve up unique experiences; rolling candles or creating cuddly teddy bears. Looking to expand your craft supplies? Visit Michaels for a variety of materials perfect for your next project or the very unique Habitat for Humanity Re-Store for a plethora of low-cost building supplies. Check the yellow pages under Arts and Crafts, or take a trip to your local craft shop for ideas on scrapbooking, stamping, beads and baubles.

ART TOURS
5701 La Jolla Blvd., La Jolla
(858) 459-5922
Birthday parties, toddler programs, after-school enrichment
programs and studio classes.

BROWN BEAR FACTORY
2375 San Diego Ave., San Diego
(877) 234-2327
Design, sew, stuff and dress your own teddy bear. Birthday parties
and tours offered.

HABITAT FOR HUMANITY RE-STORE
3653 Costa Bella St., Lemon Grove
(619) 463-0464
A unique second-hand store for building supplies, offering low-
cost materials.

I MADE IT MYSELF!
3653 Voltaire St., San Diego
(619) 224-7725
Painting, quilting, sculpting and a variety of other artistic options.
Also offers birthday parties, "Moms' Night Out" and more.

KNORR CANDLE SHOP
14906 Via de la Valle, Del Mar
(858) 755-2051
Visit the museum of candle making, try rolling a beeswax candle or
take a class.

MICHAELS
1652 Camino del Rio N., San Diego
(619) 294-589
www.michaels.com
Classes, kids club workshops and supplies. The website has a store
locator and schedule of events. Locations nationwide.

Almost Mayberry
FARMERS' MARKETS

F ew things compare to savoring a juicy peach or the scent of fresh-cut flowers. Share these delights with your family by experiencing a local farmers' market. These outdoor gatherings offer not only exceptional produce, but also a chance to meet and greet farmers—with a relaxed feel of days gone by.

Each neighborhood market varies. Some, such as Ocean Beach, offer llama rides and live music. Others have an abundance of baked goods and flowers. No matter which market you choose, let your kids plan a menu and pick out the ingredients themselves. Markets are also wonderful for festive decorations, such as pumpkins and Christmas wreaths.

A partial listing of San Diego area markets follows, but contact the San Diego County Farm Bureau website for complete up-to-date information (www.sdfarmbureau.org) or call them at (760) 745-3023.

CHULA VISTA FARMER'S MARKET
Third Ave. and Center St., Chula Vista
Thu, 3 pm—7 pm.

CORONADO FARMER'S MARKET,
First and B Sts. at Ferry Landing, Coronado
Tue, 2:30 pm—6 pm.

DEL MAR FARMER'S MARKET
Corner of Camino Del Mar and 10th St.
(City Hall parking lot), Del Mar
Sat, 1 pm—4 pm.

HILLCREST FARMER'S MARKET
Corner of Normal St. and Cleveland Ave.
(DMV parking lot), San Diego
Sun, 9 am–noon.

LA JOLLA FARMER'S MARKET
Girard Ave. and Genter St. (La Jolla Elementary School
playground), La Jolla
Sun, 9 am–1 pm.

LA MESA FARMER'S MARKET
8300 block of Allison Ave., La Mesa
Fri, 3 pm–6 pm.

OCEAN BEACH FARMER'S MARKET
4900 Newport Ave., San Diego
Wed, 4 pm–7 pm.

In a Spin
ICE AND ROLLER RINKS

In addition to myriad outdoor possibilities for in-line and roller skating in sunny San Diego, don't neglect the indoor arenas that keep good times rolling regardless of the weather. The chilly thrill of ice-skating is an excellent treat for tykes who don't see much cold weather.

Most of the locales listed offer lessons, special sessions, roller or ice hockey leagues, birthday party packages, and other family-friendly programs. Rollerskateland is always pumped with popular music, colorful lights and disco balls, in addition to laser tag and video games. The Ice Chalet in University Towne Center provides visitors with a year-round

Christmas-like atmosphere. The Ice Rink in Horton Square is a seasonal treat (December through mid-January only) offering open air skating in the glittery Gaslamp.

All establishments charge admission and rent skates. Most floor rinks allow you to bring both in-line and roller skates, but call ahead for details. Check the yellow pages under Skating for additional places that will put you "in a spin."

ICE CHALET
University Towne Centre
4545 La Jolla Village Dr., La Jolla
(858) 452-9110
Sunday "Family Day" special rates. Birthday parties, skating lessons, hockey leagues, and broomball.

THE ICE RINK IN HORTON SQUARE
255 Broadway, San Diego
(619) 234-1031 or (858) 530-1826
Seasonal outdoor skating in the city on a 100-by-60-foot rink. Family skating, "Skate with Santa" and skating school.

ROLLERSKATELAND
626 L St., Chula Vista (619) 420-4761
9365 Mission Gorge Rd., Santee (619) 562-3790.
Birthday parties, laser tag, arcade, lessons and roller hockey.

SAN DIEGO ICE ARENA
11048 Ice Skate Place, San Diego
(858) 530-1825
Hockey and figure skating lessons for ages 3 and up. Birthday parties, arcade and group discounts.

SKATEWORLD
6907 Linda Vista Rd., San Diego
(619) 560-9349
Birthday parties, arcade and lessons.

SKATE SAN DIEGO
700 E. 24th St., National City
(619) 474-1000
Birthday parties and special sessions on the large rink.

Priceless Pieces
PLACES TO PAINT POTTERY

L et your little ones be artist extraordinaires, without creating a huge mess in your own home. At these creative corners, unpainted ceramics await your artistic embellishment and start at about $6 (some studios also charge an hourly fee). Kids and adults can pick from vases, mugs, platters and more. The store supplies the paint, brushes, stencils and sponges, while you supply the ideas. The studio then glazes and fires your pieces for pick up about a week later. The following places to paint pottery have also become a popular destination for birthday parties. Look in the phone book under Ceramics for additional possibilities.

CERAMICAFE
5500 Grossmont Center Dr., La Mesa (619) 466-4800
12925 El Camino Real, Del Mar (858) 259-9958

CLAYTIME CERAMICS
1863 Bacon St., San Diego
(619) 223-6050

COLOR ME MINE
7007 Friars Rd., San Diego
(619) 220-8989 or (877) COLORME

Rev 'Em Up
RECREATION CENTERS

K ids keep active through park and recreation programs all over San Diego. Whether it's playing soccer, mastering a martial art or trying out tap dancing, recreation centers provide space for fun and active learning opportunities for all ages.

Varied and affordable programs are offered at over fifty recreation centers in the city. Many sites host after-school programs and summer camps, with learn-to-swim and field trip opportunities. From preschool to senior citizen sports, crafts and more, recreation centers are a vital part of the community.

To find complete location and contact information, visit www.sannet.gov or call (619) 525-8219 for the City of San Diego centers. Also refer to the government listing pages in the phone book. Area cities such as Chula Vista, La Mesa and El Cajon maintain their own recreation centers. Find the city name first, then look for Parks and Recreation or Recreation.

Kid Cool
SKATEBOARD PARKS

In Southern California skateboarding rules, so there are plenty of places kids can work on their moves. Comprised of asphalt or concrete ramps and bowls, half pipes, rails and other features, the parks generally require pads and helmets and are supervised and safe. Some sites charge a fee or require a membership, while others are free. In-line skates are allowed in some parks with some offering beginner areas. Call ahead if possible to verify hours and rules.

BORED? SKATE PARK
425 Imperial Beach Blvd., Imperial Beach
Indoor facility, fee, helmet and pads required.

CARLSBAD SKATE PARK
2560 Orion Way, Carlsbad
Free, beginner's area, helmet and pads required.

ESCONDIDO SPORTS CENTER
333 Bear Valley Pkwy., Escondido
(760) 738-5425
20,000 square foot indoor facility, fee, helmet and pads required.

ROBB FIELD SKATEBOARD PARK
2525 Bacon St., San Diego
(619) 531-1563
Fee, helmet and pads required.

WASHINGTON STREET SKATE PARK
Foot of Washington St. in Mission Hills, San Diego
Free, outdoors, helmet and pads required.

WOODGLENN VISTA SKATE POCKET
10250 Woodglenn Vista Rd., Santee
(619) 258-4180
Free outdoor facility, helmets and pads required.

YMCA KRAUSE FAMILY SKATE PARK
3250 Camino del Rio N., San Diego
(619) 298-3576
Large outdoor facility, fee, beginner's area, helmet and pads required.

Splish Splash
SWIMMING POOLS
AND SURF LESSONS

D on't have a pool of your own? Don't sweat it! Visit a public pool to cool off, take a lesson, or get some exercise. The City of San Diego operates more than a dozen pools, staffed with Red Cross certified lifeguards and instructors. From toddler classes to youth swim teams to lifeguard training—there's something for all ages and abilities.

Some pools can even be rented for birthday parties or gatherings. For pool locations, check the city website (www.sannet.gov), click on Parks and Recreation Department, then Recreation Centers and Pools, or call the Swim Hotline at (619) 685-1322. A few city and other pools are listed below. Find more through the YMCA or in the yellow pages under Swimming.

Mastered swimming and ready to hit the waves?

Surfing lessons can be found year-round along San Diego's coast, from private instruction to youth summer camps. Check the resources below, or inquire at a local surf shop.

Pools

ALLIED GARDENS POOL
6707 Glenroy, San Diego
(619) 235-1143

BUD KEARNS POOL
2221 Morley Dr., San Diego
(619) 692-4920

CITY HEIGHTS SWIM CENTER
4380 Landis St., San Diego
(619) 641-6125

CLAIREMONT POOL
3600 Clairemont Dr., San Diego
(858) 581-9923

LA MESA MUNICIPAL POOL
4975 Memorial Dr., La Mesa
(619) 466-4177

MISSION BEACH PLUNGE
3115 Ocean Front Walk, San Diego
(858) 488-3110

TIERRASANTA COMMUNITY POOL
11238 Clairemont Mesa Blvd., San Diego
(858) 636-4837

Surfing

MISSION BAY SPORTCENTER
1010 Santa Clara Place, San Diego
(858) 488-1004
sportcenter.com
Instruction in all water sports including surfing, sailing, water
skiing and more. Summer youth camps.

OCEAN BEACH SURF SHOP
4885 Newport Ave., San Diego
(619) 225-0674
www.ocean-experience.net
Private or group lessons and youth surf camp.

PACIFIC BEACH SURF SHOP
747 Pacific Beach Dr., San Diego
(858) 488-9575
Private or group lessons and youth surf camp.

CHAPTER 3

PLACES TO PLAY

Introduction

What do you want to do today? Scale a rock wall? Putt a colorful ball through Cinderella's castle? Take a plunge down roaring white water? Or perhaps build a sandcastle at the beach? Whatever your pleasure, "America's Finest City" has no shortage of places where your family can play all day.

In this chapter, you'll discover an array of frolicsome finds both indoors and out. Knott's Soak City Water Park promises a sliding, splashing good time. Belmont Park serves up a little bit of Coney Island, and Family Fun Center beckons children with miniature golf, arcades, batting cages and go-karts. Just as tempting, La Jolla Shores teases tykes with gentle waves, sand to sculpt and shells to find. And at Seaport Village, visitors can fly kites along the water or mount vintage carousel horses. So pack up the van and head out to enjoy all of these places to play.

A *Little Bit of Coney*
BELMONT PARK

3146 Mission Blvd., San Diego
(858) 488-1549

Tucked right next to the glittering Pacific, you'll find the curving white tracks of the historic Giant Dipper, a wooden roller coaster built in 1925. The Dipper is the cornerstone of Belmont Park and is located in Mission Beach, directly next to the action-packed boardwalk with the sand and surf beyond. There's also a carousel and raucous bumper cars, "Tilt-A-Whirl," and a few other carnival-type rides well suited for kids ten years and under. A large arcade is packed with video games and other 21st century amusements. With food choices galore and some shopping too, it's a pleasant way to spend a lazy summer evening.

Belmont Park is also home to The Plunge, open for indoor swimming, and Pirate's Cove (858-539-7474), an indoor child-sized buccaneer's adventure with ropes and nets to climb, balls to submerge into and tunnels to explore. Rent bikes or in-line skates nearby at Mission Beach Club (page 157) and cruise the boardwalk in true South California style.

SEASONS AND TIMES
➻ Year-round: Sun—Thu, 11 am—8 pm; Fri—Sat, 11 am—10 pm.

COST
➤ Admission: Free. Rides: $2 to $4 each.

GETTING THERE
➤ By car, from Interstate 5, exit at West Mission Bay Dr. and continue west to Mission Blvd. Turn south. Free parking on site. About 10 minutes from Old Town.
➤ By public transit, take bus route 34 and get off at West Mission Bay Dr. and Mission Blvd. stop.
➤ By bike, from Sports Arena Blvd. or West Point Loma Blvd., go west on Mission Bay Dr. Follow to Mission Blvd.

NEARBY
➤ SeaWorld, Mission Bay Park.

COMMENT
➤ Plan a 2-hour visit. "Family Night" specials during summer, call for specifics.

Fun in the Sun
FAMILY BEACHES

J ust pack sunscreen, beach toys, snacks, water and a book or two, and your entire family can enjoy a day on the seashore. In San Diego, there are a plethora of beaches to choose from. The following is a sampling of the best-suited beaches for families. Generally the tides are gentle, the sand is clean and there are restrooms and life-guards on-hand. Mission Bay Park (page 122) is a pleasant, surf-less alternative to the ocean. For San Diego surf, weather and water quality information, call (619) 221-8824 or (619) 289-1212.

CORONADO MUNICIPAL BEACH
Ocean Blvd. and Marina Ave., Coronado
(619) 435-4179

DEL MAR CITY BEACH
Powerhouse Park, Coast Blvd. at 15th St., Del Mar
(858) 755-1556

LA JOLLA SHORES
Camino del Oro off Ardath Rd., La Jolla
(619) 221-8900

MOONLIGHT BEACH
Fourth and B St., Encinitas
(760) 633-2880

OCEANSIDE CITY BEACH
Ocean Blvd. and Pacific St., Oceanside
(760) 435-3388

SILVER STRAND STATE BEACH
5000 Hwy. 75, Coronado
(619) 435-5184

Play All Day
FAMILY FUN CENTERS

6999 Clairemont Mesa Blvd., San Diego (858) 560-4211
1155 Graves Ave., El Cajon (619) 593-1155
830 Dan Way, Escondido (619) 741-1326
1525 W. Vista Way, Vista (760) 945-9474

Definitely not a misnomer, this place is jam-packed with fun activities for your entire brood. At any of the Family Fun Center's four locations, you can play miniature golf, speed around a go-kart track and enjoy mild carnival rides at the "Kids County Fair." Kids get a

kick out of the bumper boats, where you hop
aboard a motorized tube equipped with water
blasters to squirt your neighbor. At each location,
you'll find arcade games, batting cages and a kid-
friendly restaurant called Bullwinkle's that serves
hot dogs and pizza.

Although the sites differ slightly—each putt-putt
course is different and some Centers offer soft
activity gyms and laser tag—all Family Fun Center
locations specialize in providing an exceptionally
clean and friendly environment. Not surprising,
birthday parties are a big deal. Group discounts and
special package deals are available—call for information on current promotions.

SEASONS AND TIMES
➤ Year-round: Mon–Thu, 11 am–11 pm; Fri, 11 am–midnight; Sat,
10 am–midnight; Sun, 10 am–11 pm. Subject to change, call for
confirmation.

COST
➤ Complete access wristbands: $13 or $23, call for details.
Miniature golf: $6.50 per person per game, undeer 6 free. Go-
karts and bumper boats: $5.50 per person. Carnival rides: $2.50
each. Arcade games: 25 to 75 cents each.

GETTING THERE
➤ To Clairemont Mesa Blvd. location by car, from Hwy.163 or
Interstate 8, travel on Interstate 805 north to Clairemont Mesa
Blvd. Exit East. The center is immediately to the south. Free
parking. About 15 minutes from Old Town. Call for directions to
other locations.
➤ By public transit, take bus route 5 to stop at Clairemont Mesa
Blvd. at Clairemont Dr. Pick up bus 25 to Clairemont Mesa Blvd.
and Shawline stop. Walk east.

COMMENT
➤ Plan a 3-hour visit. Diaper-changing facilities available. Most
areas wheelchair accessible.

Jumpin' Jive
INDOOR GYMS

Cartwheel into one of these kids' gyms, where the emphasis is on tumbling, stretching, and motor skill building amidst colorful kid-sized mats, soft slides, climbing nets and playful equipment that builds physical ability and a "can-do" attitude. With music and merriment, instructors guide kids through activities that instill an appreciation for physical fitness that can last a lifetime. And while the kids enjoy good healthy fun, they also develop coordination, agility and confidence. Most sites offer programs for infants through age twelve, and host craft nights, birthday parties, movie nights, Parents' Night Out and more. Call each location for details about their specific programming.

GYMINNY KIDS
11501 Rancho Bernardo Dr., San Diego
(858) 451-0204

ISLAND TUMBLE
1009 C Ave., Coronado
(619) 435-7262

JW TUMBLES
104-12205 Scripps Poway Pkwy., San Diego (858) 566-4657
12750 Carmel Country Rd., San Diego (858) 481-5576
2522 Jamacha Rd., El Cajon (619) 670-6212
www.jwtumbles.com

MY GYM
12125 Alta Carmel Court, San Diego
(858) 487-4961
www.my-gym.com

Reach the Peak
INDOOR ROCK CLIMBING

When your children have energy to burn, venture to an indoor climbing gym where they can literally climb the walls. These state-of-the-art facilities encourage kids to climb (and even offer birthday party packages), but also cater to professional climbers who come in to tighten their skills. And while kids savor the challenge of climbing, they are also developing strength, balance, flexibility and coordination.

With an emphasis on safety, these facilities hire CPR and first aid certified staff and use the highest quality apparatus. For regular climbers, memberships are available and the routes are always changing for a new challenge. For first-timers or adventurous families who want to give it a go, day passes cost about $10 and all necessary equipment can be rented at low cost, with professional instructors to get you started.

If you're truly interested in taking up the sport, there are private and group lessons available, providing confidence and skills before heading out to the real hills. Inquire about group discounts, birthday parties and Scout badge programs.

SOLID ROCK GYM
2074 Hancock St., San Diego (619) 299-1124
13026 Stowe Dr., Poway (619) 299-1124 (open weekends only.)
www.solidrockgym.com

VERTICAL HOLD
9580 Distribution Ave., San Diego (858) 586-7572
www.verticalhold.com

Surf's Up at
KNOTT'S SOAK CITY

2052 Entertainment Circle, Chula Vista
(619) 661-7373

Amidst attractions like Banzai and Point Break, who wouldn't be excited? Step into a city seemingly all its own—and prepare for slippery good time. Knott's Soak City is a water park with 16 tube, body and speed slides (height and age restrictions apply). But rest assured, while the most adventurous of the family will be occupied with these thrill slides, there's something for everyone.

Small children love Tyke's Trough, a scaled-down waterfall wonderland with slides and pools that are off-limits to older kids. Kids adore Dick's Beach House, a three-story playland set in a foot of water and equipped with climbing nets, crawling tubes and of course, water cannons, faucets, nozzles and a giant bucket of water overhead.

Families looking to spend time together can enjoy Balboa Bay wave pool with a shallow end and rafts to ride. The Coronado Express is a 78-foot tall, 668-foot long white water raft adventure that everyone loves. And at a lazy Sunset River, your bunch can float round-and-round on a gentle, refreshing waterway.

Although you can't bring in your own food, there is an array of excellent eateries. Lifeguards are always on duty and the park is stocked with life vests in all sizes to borrow (at no charge). Changing rooms and all necessary rafts and tubes are also provided free, but there is a small locker rental fee. Knott's Soak City offers group discounts, season passes and birthday party packages.

SEASONS AND TIMES
➺ Memorial Day—Labor Day: Daily, 10 am—8 pm. May and Sept: Weekends only. Hours vary, call for confirmation.

COST
➺ Adults $21.95, children (3 to 11) $14.95, under 3 free.

GETTING THERE
➺ By car, travel Interstate 5 south to Main St. Head east for 5 miles. Entrance to the south. Parking $5. About 30 minutes from Old Town.

NEARBY
➺ Chula Vista Nature Center.

COMMENT
➺ Plan at least a 4-hour visit.

Flying High
SEAPORT VILLAGE

849 W. Harbor Dr., San Diego
(619) 235-4014

Dozens of unique stores make up most of Seaport Village, although its picturesque waterfront setting makes it more alluring than most malls. With early 1900s charm, cobbled paths wind through candy and cookie shops, a magic shop, kite store, a trove of nautical treasures and many more family-friendly merchants.

Beyond shopping, the video arcade and 1890 Broadway Flying Horses Carousel are a treat, and neighboring Embarcadero Marina Park is primo for kite flying. Balloon-twisting clowns and a strolling mime make for a memorable day. Nobody will go hungry as edible selections abound, from the humble hot dog to sushi. While near the marina, peek at the luxurious yachts in the harbor where children enjoy learning the vessels' names and home ports. Cinderella Carriage Company (page 162) departs from Seaport Village for a horse-drawn appreciation of the city and the ferry glides folks across the bay to Coronado Island (page 17). Cruise bikes or in-line skates along the waterfront sidewalk south to reach the Embarcadero.

SEASONS AND TIMES
➤ Sept—May: Daily, 10 am—9 pm. June—Aug: Daily, 10 am—10 pm.

COST
➤ Free. Carousel $1.

GETTING THERE
➤ By car, follow Interstate 5 south to the Front St. Exit. Turn west on Ash St., south on Pacific Hwy. and follow to the entrance. From Hwy. 163 south, Exit Ash St. Turn south on Pacific Hwy. and follow to the entrance. Parking $2/hr or free with validated purchase. About 15 minutes from Old Town.
➤ By public transit, take bus route 34 and get off at Broadway and Kettner stop. By trolley, take the Blue Line to American Plaza Trolley Station. Then ride the Orange Line to Seaport Village Station. Cross Harbor Dr. to entrance.

NEARBY
➤ Gaslamp Quarter, Maritime Museum, Coronado.

COMMENT
➤ Plan a 2-hour visit.

Zap! You're it at
ULTRAZONE

3146 Sports Arena Blvd., San Diego
(619) 221-0100

Enter the surreal feel of Ultrazone, the ultimate laser tag game. Lose youself in an imaginary landscape of the future (two levels) where you must zap or be zapped in this high-tech version of the old favorite—tag. Here, you don vests and grab a blaster, then play in teams to defend certain areas of the terrain. You'll scramble through mazes, over ramps and other features.

Children must be seven or older to play. Ultrazone staff will assist younger players, but otherwise, go as a family group and expect timid tykes to stick close. One of the best things about this game of tag is that you're never out of the game, just unable to blast for a few seconds after you've been hit. Birthday parties, group discounts, memberships and annual passes available.

SEASONS AND TIMES
➤ Year-round: Mon—Thu, 4 pm—11 pm; Fri, 2 pm—2 am; Sat, 10 am—2 pm; Sun, 10 am—11 pm. Extended summer hours, call to confirm.

COST
➤ Adults and children $6.50 per game. Children (under 11) $5.50 on Sat—Sun,10 am—2 pm.

GETTING THERE
➤ By car, from Hwy. 163 take Interstate 8 east to Rosecrans St. Exit. At Sports Arena Blvd. (third light), turn west. On-site parking. About 5 minutes from Old Town.
➤ By public transit, take bus route 26.
➤ By bike, take Mission Bay Dr. south to Sports Arena Blvd east or pedal West Point Loma Blvd. north to Sports Arena Blvd. east.

NEARBY
➤ Old Town, Presidio Park, Solid Rock Gym.

COMMENT
➤ Games last 15 minutes. Wear dark clothes unless you want to "glow." No sandals or tank tops.

OTHER PLACES TO PLAY

BARNES TENNIS CENTER
4490 West Point Loma Blvd., San Diego
(619) 221-9000
Kids play free. Summer camps, private and group lessons. Sand
volleyball courts.Year-round: Daily. Call for current prices and
hours.

BATTER'S BOX
12576 Kirkham Court, Poway
(877) 822-6228
Indoor batting facility with seven baseball and five softball
pitching machines. Lessons, team discounts and birthday parties.
Year-round: Mon—Fri, 11 am—9 pm; Sat—Sun, 9 am—7 pm. Call for
prices.

PRESIDIO HILLS GOLF COURSE
4136 Wallace St., San Diego
(619) 295-9476
Nine-hole course offering classes for children, private instruction
and a summer camp program. Year-round: Daily. Call for current
hours and prices.

QUALCOMM STADIUM
9449 Friars Rd., San Diego
(619) 641-3100
Hosts professional sports (including the San Diego Chargers), and
other events like motocross and monster truck rallies.

THE BOARDWALK
1286 Fletcher Pkwy., El Cajon
(619) 449-7800
www.boardwalk-parkway.com
Indoor amusement center with arcade games, a carousel, coaster,
soft play gym and more. Year-round: Sun—Thu, 11 am—10:30 pm;
Fri—Sat, 11 am—midnight. Games and rides: 5 cents to $1.50.

CHAPTER 4

PLACES TO LEARN

Introduction

With over 90 museums and historical sites in San Diego County, this chapter introduces you to only a few of many mindexpanding explorations that will keep your family engaged, imagining and learning.

Discover how water evaporates at the Aquarium, or control a mock space shuttle at the Science Center. Take to the stage at the Museum of Making Music, or if you'd rather, sign up for a class at the Art Museum. Aspiring engineers enjoy the Model Railroad Museum where you can take charge at the Toy Train Gallery. Step back in time and dress up Egyptian style at the Museum of Man. For fairy-tale fun, visit the Children's Discovery Museum of North County. Have a little paleontologist in your family? Head to the Natural History Museum and learn all about the fossils and plants of Southern California.

For more educational fun, try one of the other sites suggested at the end of this chapter. No matter what you choose to do, intrepid families will enjoy an ever-expanding array of learning possibilities at these kid-friendly places.

Sea Wonders
BIRCH AQUARIUM
AT SCRIPPS

**2300 Expedition Way, La Jolla
(858) 534-FISH
www.aquarium.ucsd.edu**

An extension of the Scripps Institute of Oceanography, this stunning interpretive center is perched above the Pacific on chaparral-covered cliffs. Inside, varied marine habitats showcase species sure to fascinate youngsters; giant lobsters, anemones, sea horses, jellyfish and colorful tropical fish are particularly pleasing.

"Please touch" signs throughout the facility invite little hands to feel the shell of a mounted giant clam or a cluster of mussels. In the Explore the Blue Planet oceanography museum area, over a dozen interactive exhibits tempt children's curiosity—learn how water evaporates, why water conducts electricity and how waves and cold fronts are formed. There is even a mock grocery store where kids "scan" household items and learn how the ocean contributed to the creation of many common products. The simulated submarine ride takes folks for a quick dip. At the earthquake area, discover interesting facts about plate tectonics and sea-floor spreading. You'll also see a working seismograph and get to hop aboard a shaking stand, to get a feel of what "Richter" really means.

The human-made tide pools on the patio are for viewing only, although there's a supervised handling area open most weekends and during summer. Food carts in the front plaza area offer drinks and snacks. The impressive education department maintains a variety of on-site and outreach programs, including summer camps and material for teachers. Have a themed birthday party where tykes learn about sharks, whales or tide pool treasures while they celebrate.

SEASONS AND TIMES
➤ Year-round: Daily, 9 am—5 pm. Closed Thanksgiving, Christmas and New Year's.

COST
➤ Adults $8.50, seniors (over 59) $7.50, children (3 to 17) $5, under 2 free.

GETTING THERE
➤ By car, take Interstate 5 north, exit La Jolla Village Dr. and head west. Drive one mile to Expedition Way and follow the signs. Pay parking available. About 25 minutes from Old Town.
➤ By public transit, take bus route 34 to North Torrey Pines Rd. Walk north to Expedition Way.
➤ By bike, travel Torrey Pines Rd. north to Expedition Way.

NEARBY
➤ La Jolla Shores, Children's Pool/La Jolla Cove, Torrey Pines State Reserve.

COMMENT
➤ Plan a 2-hour visit. Diaper-changing facilities available.

Knights and Damsels
CHILDREN'S DISCOVERY MUSEUM OF NORTH COUNTY

300 Carlsbad Village Dr., Suite 103, Carlsbad
(760) 720-0737
www.museumforchildren.org

Small, but bursting at the seams with activity and creativity, the Children's Discovery Museum was designed specifically with kids (aged two to ten) in mind. Everything, except the fun, is scaled down to "pint size."

Children flock to Castle Play, a replica of a medieval castle, where there are princesses' gowns, kings' robes and knights' armor to be donned. Kid's Marketplace is stocked with groceries, shopping carts and a real, working checkout counter. Tiny employees will appreciate the aprons and the produce scale, and Mom and Dad will appreciate the food pyramid station that teaches nutritional lessons.

Visit World of Sound to sample multicultural instruments mounted on a giant map of the world. Fishing Boat sets children sailing to fish for magnetic yellowtail and the Solar Power exhibit proves the sun's ability to power a toy train. There are also exciting, ever-changing art projects to be done in the Creativity Corner, and toddlers will find fun with "magic" mirrors and other wonders in their own soft-sculpted area.

Don't miss the Bubble Tube, where kids can check out a giant bubble from the inside. The Children's Discovery Museum offers birthday party packages and annual passes.

SEASONS AND TIMES
➥ Year-round: Sun, Tue—Thu, 12 pm—5 pm; Fri—Sat, 10 am—5 pm. Call for extended summer hours.

COST
➥ Adults and children $4, under 2 free.

GETTING THERE
➥ By car, from Interstate 5 heading north, exit Carlsbad Village Dr. and turn west. Travel half a mile to Village Fair Shopping Center on the north side. The Museum is located in the northwest corner of the interior courtyard. About 50 minutes from Old Town.
➥ By public transit, take bus route 34 from Old Town Transit Center to North Torrey Pines Rd., then North County Transit Bus 301 to Carlsbad Blvd. Walk west to Village Faire Shopping Center.

NEARBY
➥ Legoland, Carlsbad Flower Fields, Museum of Making Music.

COMMENT
➥ Plan a 1-hour visit. The restrooms are located on the upper level of the shopping center; ask for the key at the Museum admission counter.

Feel the Beat?
MUSEUM OF
MAKING MUSIC

5790 Armada Dr., Carlsbad
(877) 551-9976
www.museumofmakingmusic.org

You'll never find a "Quiet Please" sign at this museum, where singing and dancing are encouraged. Take a walk through exhibits honoring American music, from 1890 to the present day. You'll experience the We'll Try Anything Years (1930–1949) and encounter Benny Goodman and the sound of swing. Be-bop through The Baby Boom Sparks Dynamic Growth (1950-1969) and listen and learn about Elvis Presley, Ray Charles and the Beatles.

Kids like the kiosks where they press buttons and hear popular tunes from 1909 through the heydays of rag, blues, jazz and folk music. Along the way, some 450 instruments are displayed, including an autographed Steinway piano, a few of Bo Diddley's customized guitars and 1890 "potato bug" mandolin. There are also gorgeous horns, harmonicas and other vintage pieces, such as a theremin (an odd-looking instrument that produced the creepy sounds of early horror movies and sci-fi flicks).

Point out to tykes and teens the CD's predecessor—the 1898 Graphophone phonograph. Kids flip when they find the World Turned Upside Down

(1970–1989) exhibit because they get to mount the stage (with a mural of rock group KISS just behind) and join the band at this interactive sound stage. It comes complete with electric drums, keyboard and guitar. While they hear hits via headphones, they play along by tapping the sticks, rattling the keys and wailing on a guitar, just like the stars. Of course, kids of all ages are encouraged to jam, and the Museum Store has a few playable pieces, too.

SEASONS AND TIMES
➤ Year-round: Tue—Sun, 10 am—5 pm. Closed Thanksgiving, Christmas, New Year's and Independence Day.

COST
➤ Adults $5, seniors (over 64), active military with ID, children (4 to 18) $3, under 4 free.

GETTING THERE
➤ By car, travel Interstate 5 north to Cannon Rd. and turn east. Go to Legoland Dr. and turn south. At the traffic circle, follow the signs onto Armada Dr. Located in the NAMM building on the south side of the street. Free parking. About 45 minutes from Old Town.
➤ By public transit, take the Coaster to Poinsettia Station, then bus route 344 to Armada Dr.

NEARBY
➤ Carlsbad Flower Fields, Children's Discovery Museum of North County, Legoland.

COMMENT
➤ Annual passes, a Girl Scout badge program and group discounts available.

Cavemen, Crafts and Scarabs
MUSEUM OF MAN

1350 El Prado in Balboa Park, San Diego
(619) 239-2001
www.museumofman.org

Within the walls of this anthropological museum, children are immediately spellbound. Kids are fascinated to learn how people have evolved, found food and shelter, raised families, run societies, celebrated life and addressed death through the ages. Be prepared for the many questions your children will have after visiting the Museum of Man.

Youngsters love the toys, jewelry, pottery and baby papoose of the Kumeyaay (Native people to the San Diego region). At Life and Death on the Nile, examine Egyptian daily life, including such rare artifacts as a 3,000 year-old coffin, intricately detailed mummy masks and sacred amulets. Among the most intriguing areas for children is the Early Man exhibit, where visitors enter a cave (complete with paintings) and view dioramas filled with life-sized models depicting the evolution of humans. There are fossils and stone tools as well.

Consider saving the best exhibit for last. The Children's Discovery Center in the Museum of Man presents Discover Egypt, where kids can enter an Egyptian noble's home, dress up in costumes, play ancient games and decipher hieroglyphic messages. Kids and playful parents can build a pyramid from wooden blocks, or visit a replica of a present-day archeological field camp.

Wednesday through Sunday, the Museum hosts weaving and tortilla-making demonstrations. The education department offers something for all ages, including preschool classes, Scout badge programs, outreach presentations and teacher resources. Annual passes and group discounts available. Some exhibits may not be suitable for young children. If you have concerns, check with the admission desk.

SEASONS AND TIMES
➤ Year-round: Daily, 10 am—4:30 pm. Closed Thanksgiving, Christmas and New Year's.

COST
➤ Adults $6, children (6 to 17) $3, under 6 free.

GETTING THERE
➤ By car, from Interstate 5 south, exit Sassafras and take Laurel St. east into Balboa Park. From Hwy. 163, head south to Park Blvd. Turn north, follow the signs. Enter at Village Place, walk the Prado west. About 10 minutes from Old Town.
➤ By public transit, take bus route 7/7A/7B to stop at Park Blvd. and Village Place. Walk west down the Prado.
➤ By bike, follow car directions from Park Blvd., or take Sixth Ave. and enter Balboa Park at Laurel St.

NEARBY
➤ Model Railroad Museum, Natural History Museum, Reuben H. Fleet Science Center, San Diego Museum of Art, Old Globe Theatre, Junior Theatre, Starlight Bowl, San Diego Zoo.

COMMENT
➤ Plan a 1- to 2-hour visit.

Blast Off!
REUBEN H. FLEET SCIENCE CENTER

1875 El Prado in Balboa Park, San Diego
(619) 238-1233
www.rhfleet.org

The Fleet Science Center, light-years ahead of many other learning centers, has dozens of interactive exhibits spread over five galleries. ExploraZone takes over the main exhibit floor until 2003, presenting over 30 changing hands-on discovery displays that examine relationships between science, art, math and human perception. Color Shadows lets families experiment with light and color. About Faces provides families with an opportunity to "make a face" and alter the image with mirrors, graphics and computers. Meteor Storm tosses you into virtual reality, where you'll race through space and blast meteors. At the Signals exhibit, you'll study the transmission of information—from the use of sound tubes to the Internet.

The Little Learners Lab will pique your youngsters' interest, while the SciTours simulator ride attracts older kids. In the Challenger Learning Center, control a mock space shuttle mission (reservations required). The Fleet Science Center also houses the only IMAX™ domed theater in California, so don't miss taking in a big screen show.

Sky Tonight Planetarium shows are held once a month (call for details). The education department offers day camps, teacher workshops and other programs. Annual passes and group discounts available.

SEASONS AND TIMES

➤ Year-round: Daily, Sun–Thu, 9:30 am–5 pm (Wed until 7 pm); Fri–Sat, 9:30 am–9 pm. Call for current IMAX™ and Planetarium showtimes.

COST

➤ Exhibit Galleries only: Adults $6.50, seniors (over 65) $5.50, children (3 to 12) $5, under 3 free. Galleries and IMAX™ film: Adults $11, seniors (over 65) $9, children (3 to 12) $8. SciTours included in both options. Planetarium shows: Adults $6.50, seniors (65 and older) $5, juniors (under 13) $5.50.

GETTING THERE

➤ By car, from Interstate 5 south take Pershing Dr. Exit, then follow Florida Dr. west. Follow Zoo Place west to Park Blvd. Turn south and proceed to Space Theatre Way, turn west. From Hwy. 163 south, exit Park Blvd. and head north. Turn west at Space Theater Way. About 10 minutes from Old Town.

➤ By public transit, take bus route 7/7A/7B to stop at Park Blvd. and Village Place. Museum is on south side of the fountain.

NEARBY

➤ Model Railroad Museum, Natural History Museum, Museum of Man, San Diego Museum of Art, Old Globe Theater, Junior Theater, Starlight Bowl, San Diego Zoo.

COMMENT

➤ Plan a 2-hour visit. Diaper changing facilities on-site.

Charming Choo-Choos
SAN DIEGO MODEL RAILROAD MUSEUM

1649 El Prado in Balboa Park, San Diego
(619) 696-0199
www.sdmodelrailroadm.com

To kids, there's nothing better than a whistle blowing, chug-chugging choo-choo train. At the Model Railroad Museum, every child's fantasy is fulfilled, as one of the largest collections of model trains in the world whiz along the tracks in four exhibits displaying California railroads.

There's Telechapi Pass and the Cabrillo-Southwestern Scale Exhibit, the Pacific Desert Lines and the San Diego & Arizona Eastern—including awesome Carriso Gorge and Goat Canyon Trestle. The intricately detailed landscapes include model houses, warehouses and ranches, historic buildings, cars and people. Look carefully. You'll soon be chuckling at the creators' wit. Engineers man the tracks and are usually available for questions.

Visit the Toy Train Gallery near the back of the building, where children try their hand at guiding Lionel engines over the tracks and through tunnels. A small wooden hand-powered train set entices the youngest. There are educational displays and several artifacts, such as a flashing-crossing signal. The gift shop has lots of goodies for train-lovers and the Pacific Beach Room can be rented for special events and birthday parties. The Museum is located in the lower level of Casa de Balboa in Balboa Park, accessible by stairs or elevator.

SEASONS AND TIMES
➻ Year-round: Tue—Fri, 11 am—4 pm; Sat—Sun, 11 am—5 pm. Closed Thanksgiving and Christmas.

COST
➻ Adults $4, seniors (over 59) $3, students and military w/ID $2.50, under 15 free when accompanied by an adult.

GETTING THERE
➻ By car, from Interstate 5 south, exit Sassafras St. and follow to Laurel St. Turn west on Laurel and continue into Balboa Park. From Hwy. 163 south, exit Park Blvd. and head north. Enter Balboa Park turning west at President's Way. About 10 minutes from Old Town.
➻ By public transit, take bus route 7/7A/7B to stop at Park Blvd. and Village Place. Walk west to El Prado.
➻ By bike, follow car directions from Sassafrass or follow Sixth Ave. to Laurel and turn west to enter Balboa Park.

NEARBY
➻ San Diego Museum of Art, Natural History Museum, Reuben H. Fleet Science Center, Junior Theatre, Museum of Man, Old Globe Theatre, San Diego Zoo, Starlight Bowl.

COMMENT
➻ Plan a 1-hour visit.

Awesome Art
SAN DIEGO
MUSEUM OF ART

1450 El Prado in Balboa Park, San Diego
(619) 232-7931
www.sdmart.org

The San Diego Museum of Art, housed in a Spanish colonial building, is not only home to fabulous works of art, but is itself a masterpiece. From its high ceilings with hand-painted beams to the regal staircase in the foyer, families can't help but be awed as they step through the door.

Inside, explore the 20 galleries filled with treasures. From the exquisite Italian Renaissance works upstairs, to quizzical contemporary wonders downstairs, there's something for every taste. Pick up a "family guide" to carry with you. These clever and constructive laminated sheets ask pointed questions about certain elements in each piece. They also provide tidbits about the cultural significance of the art in question, and are a great starting point for a family museum-going experience.

Consider bringing a pencil and pad to allow older children to sketch their favorites (make sure you fill out a permission form at the admission desk). Since the pieces are hands-off, use a stroller for your youngest (restricted only when it's very crowded). Check out the Image Gallery where you can locate works of art via computer, and print out your own copy.

The Museum hosts changing special exhibitions throughout the year in addition to their acclaimed permanent collections. The education department offers programs for all ages including classes, camps and the family-favorite Open Studio (held every Saturday from 11 am to 2 pm where painters, sculptors, ceramists and others offer free art lessons).

SEASONS AND TIMES
➤ Year-round: Tue—Sun, 10 am—6 pm (Thu until 9 pm).

COST
➤ Adults $8, seniors (over 64), students and military $6, children (6 to 17) $3, under 6 free.

GETTING THERE
➤ By car, from Interstate 5 south exit at Sassafras St. Go east at Laurel St. and drive into Balboa Park. Park in the lot on north side immediately in front of Museum. From Hwy. 163 south, exit Park Blvd. Turn north and go to President's Way. Enter the park heading west and park in area lots. About 10 minutes from Old Town.
➤ By public transit, take bus route 7/7A/7B and ride it to stop at Park Blvd. and Village Place. Walk west to El Prado.

NEARBY
➤ Natural History Museum, Reuben H. Fleet Science Center, Model Railroad Museum, Museum of Man, Old Globe Theater, Junior Theater, Starlight Bowl, San Diego Zoo.

COMMENT
➤ Plan a 1-hour visit. Backpacks and large bags must be checked upon entering. Diaper-changing facilities available.

Learning and Liking It
SAN DIEGO NATURAL HISTORY MUSEUM

1788 El Prado in Balboa Park, San Diego
(619) 232-3821
www.sdnhm.org

Learning about the world in which we live is tons of fun at the Natural History Museum. Although the museum is undergoing renovations and expansion, there's still plenty to see and do. New permanent and special exhibits examining varying aspects of our natural world will be opening over the next few years.

Natural Treasures: Past and Present teaches about rocks, fossils, plants and animals of Southern and Baja California, through engaging (often touchable) displays. Of course, one of the most kid-intriguing exhibits, the rattlesnake habitat, is hands-off! Planned special exhibitions will include T. Rex on Trial, where visitors must sleuth out the truth using fossil evidence—was *Tyrannosaurus Rex* guilty of being a ravenous predator?

The Discovery Room houses live animals, as well as rocks, fossils and other natural objects for handling, in addition to providing field guides and microscopes for studious types. The Insects exhibit offer visitors a chance to see giant hissing cockroaches, tarantulas and scorpions. Journey Through the Past is a permanent exhibit area displaying dinosaurs, Ice Age mammal skeletons and walk-through, multi-sensory dioramas.

The large-format theater presents Ocean Oasis, an excellent educational tribute to the diversity of animal and plant species of Baja California and the Sea of Cortés. The education department offers classes for adults and children, outings and day camps. For a treat, Miss Frizzle™ (from the popular TV series) instructs on various topics on Wacky Science Sundays. Annual passes and group discounts available.

SEASONS AND TIMES
➤ Summer (Memorial Day–Labor Day): Daily, 9:30 am–5:30 pm. Winter (Labor Day–Memorial Day): Daily, 9:30 am–4:30 pm.

COST
➤ Adults $7, seniors, active military and college students $6, children (3 to 17) $5, under 3 free.

GETTING THERE
➤ By car, from Interstate 5 south take Pershing Dr. Exit, then follow Florida Dr. west. Travel Zoo Place west to Park Blvd. Turn south and proceed to Village Place, turning west to enter. From Hwy. 163 south, exit Park Blvd. and head north. Turn west at Village Place. About 10 minutes from Old Town.
➤ By public transit, take bus route 7/7A/7B and get off at Park Blvd. and Village Place. Museum is immediately southwest.
➤ By bike, travel Sixth Ave. to Laurel St., turn west into Balboa Park. Follow to east end of El Prado near fountain.

NEARBY
➤ Reuben H. Fleet Science Center, Model Railroad Museum, Museum of Man, San Diego Museum of Art, Old Globe Theatre, Junior Theatre, Starlight Bowl, San Diego Zoo.

COMMENT
➤ Plan on spending about 90 minutes. Diaper-changing facilities available. Call or check website for exhibit updates.

OTHER PLACES TO LEARN

ARCO U.S. OLYMPIC TRAINING CENTER
2800 Olympic Pkwy., Chula Vista
(619) 656-1500
Facility where world-class athletes train daily. Tours daily. Free.

CALIFORNIA SURF MUSEUM
223 North Coast Hwy., Oceanside
(760) 721-6876
www.surfmuseum.org
Historical photos, vintage surfboards and other artifacts relate the
history of surfing along the California coast. Year-round: Mon,
Thu—Sun, 10 am—4 pm. Free.

COMPUTER MUSEUM OF AMERICA
640 C St., San Diego
(619) 235-8222
www.computer-museum.org
An exploration of the evolution of the computer, complete with
unique artifacts and working exhibits, such as a mechanical
calculator built in 1873. Year-round: Tue—Sat, 10 am—5 pm. Adults
$2, children $1, under 2 free.

HERITAGE OF THE AMERICAS MUSEUM
12110 Cuyamaca College Dr. West, El Cajon
(619) 670-5194
A cultural and educational center featuring prehistoric, historic
art, culture (including Native American tools, weavings, and
jewelry), natural history displays and fossils. Water Conservation
Garden located nearby. Year-round: Tue—Fri, 10 am—4 pm; Sat,
noon—4 pm. Adults $3, seniors $2, students $1, under 16 free.

MARINE CORPS RECRUIT DEPOT COMMAND MUSEUM
Off Pacific Hwy., San Diego
(619) 524-6038
Discover art, medals, armory, weapons, a WWI ambulance and a
WWII Jeep. Video presentations also available. Year-round: Tue—
Fri, 8 am—4 pm; Sat, noon—4 pm. Free.

MINGEI INTERNATIONAL MUSEUM

1439 El Prado, Balboa Park, San Diego
(619) 239-0003
Traditional and contemporary folk art. Year-round: Tue—Sun, 10
am—4 pm. Adults $5, children (6 to 17) $2, under 6 free.

MUSEUM OF CONTEMPORARY ART

700 Prospect St., La Jolla
(858) 454-3541
www.mcasandiego.org
Host to changing exhibitions and a garden exhibit area. Family
programs free the first Sunday of every month. Year-round: Mon,
Tue, Thu—Sun, 11 am—5 pm. Adults $4, seniors, students and
military $2, under 12 free.

MUSEUM OF PHOTOGRAPHIC ARTS

1649 El Prado, Balboa Park, San Diego
(619) 238-7559
www.mopa.org
Five galleries of photographs and films. Year-round: Daily, 10 am—
5 pm. Adults $6, seniors, students, military and children (13 to 17)
$4, under 13 free.

SAN DIEGO AEROSPACE MUSEUM

2001 Pan American Plaza, Balboa Park, San Diego
(619) 234-8291
www.aerospacemuseum.org
See over 65 examples of air and spacecraft. From the Wright
Brothers Flyer to World War II Spitfires, this museum pays tribute
to aviation history. Year-round: Daily, 10 am—4:30 pm. Closed
Thanksgiving, Christmas, and New Year's. Adults $8, seniors $7,
children (6 to 17) $3, under 6 free.

SAN DIEGO AUTOMOTIVE MUSEUM

2080 Pan American Plaza, Balboa Park, San Diego
(619) 231-2886
Glimpse a hand-cranked Model T and a red-hot Bizzarini among
other vehicles. Year-round: Daily, 10 am—5 pm. Closed Thanksgiving, Christmas and New Year's. Adults $7, seniors and active mili-
tary $6, children (6 to 15) $3, under 6 free.

SAN DIEGO HALL OF CHAMPIONS

2131 Pan American Plaza, Balboa Park, San Diego
(619) 234-2544
www.sandiegosports.org
A multi-sport museum honoring local greats and other athletes.
Interactive exhibits test athletic skills and "white glove" tours allow
guests to see and touch artifacts. Year-round: Daily, 10 am—4:30
pm. Adults $4, seniors, students, military and children (6 to 14)
$2, under 6 free.

SAN DIEGO HISTORICAL SOCIETY MUSEUM

1649 El Prado, Balboa Park, San Diego
(619) 232-6203
www.sdhistory.com
San Diego's history is chronicled through changing and permanent
exhibits, as well as photographs. Year-round: Tue—Sun, 10 am—
4:30 pm. Adults $5, seniors, students and military $4, children (6
to 17) $2, under 6 free.

TIMKEN MUSEUM

1500 El Prado, Balboa Park, San Diego
(619) 239-5548
Paintings from European, American and Russian artists. Year-
round: Tue—Sat, 10 am—4:30 pm; Sun, 1:30—4:30 pm. Free.

CHAPTER 5

MUSIC, THEATER, DANCE & CINEMA

Introduction

San Diego steadily grows as a cultural destination. With theater groups, performing arts centers, orchestras, dance troupes and much more, there's no excuse for allowing your kids to miss the thrill and inspiration of live performance.

Many selections in this chapter not only offer sensational productions that children enjoy, but also provide instruction to young performers. San Diego Junior Theatre offers classes year-round and presents a full schedule of performances throughout the year. The unusual flair of Fern Street Circus captivates local kids—and instructs them too. Even award-winning adult professional organizations continually create enriching programs for youth. The San Diego Symphony makes classical music accessible while the City Ballet throws Sugar Plum Fairy parties and the Starlight creates magic beneath the stars. With a few special cinema showings to round out the options, you and your family can experience kid-friendly culture at these appealing performances and venues. Visit www.sandiegoperforms.com for current music, dance and theater productions in San Diego County.

Under One Roof
CALIFORNIA CENTER FOR THE ARTS

340 North Escondido Blvd., Escondido
(760) 839-4138
www.artcenter.org

This exquisite 12-acre complex opened in 1994, housing a museum, theater and concert hall. Embracing all aspects of the performing and visual arts, the Center's season schedule offers everything from Ballet Folklorico to jazz orchestras, Twyla Tharp dance troupes to performances by Penn and Teller.

Family Theater on Sunday afternoons brings a variety of performances ideally suited for children. Sometimes it's a ballet or a play—and other times it's a special kid-themed concert. Make it a day-long visit and check out the Center's museum before the show. The Museum hosts changing exhibitions, as well as kid days with art projects and other special doings. Perfect for pre-show picnicking, the Center is located next to Grape Day Park, where your family will enjoy shady trees, picnic tables and a playground. Season subscriptions available.

SEASONS AND TIMES

➤ Administration: Year-round, Tue–Fri, 8 am–5 pm. Museum: Year-round, Tue–Sat, 10 am–5 pm; Sun, noon–5 pm. Closed Mondays. Call for current performance schedules.

COST

➤ Museum: Adults $5, seniors and military $4, students and youth (13 to 18) $3, under 13 free. Shows: Between $12 to $30 per ticket per show. Family Theater: $9.50 per ticket. For tickets, call (760) 839-4100.

GETTING THERE

➤ By car, from Interstate 8 take Interstate 15 north to Valley Pkwy. east. Turn north on Escondido Blvd. About 40 minutes from Old Town.

NEARBY

➤ Wild Animal Park.

COMMENT

➤ Diaper-changing facilities available.

Magical Musicals
CHRISTIAN COMMUNITY THEATER & CHRISTIAN YOUTH THEATER

1545 Pioneer Way, El Cajon
(619) 588-0206
www.cctcyt.org

Providing some of the finest live family entertainment in all of San Diego, these two theater companies also offer youth theater training and performance opportunities for the community.

High atop Mt. Helix, Christian Community Theater (CCT) holds several productions in a picturesque outdoor amphitheater during the summer months. Favorites have included *Grease, Sound of Music* and *Cinderella*. Although you have to take a shuttle and use portable restrooms, the Mt. Helix venue is breathtaking—with its spectacular panoramic view of mountains to the east and the Pacific to west. Bring snacks and a toy or two to keep your youngest entertained.

The Christian Youth Theater (CYT) stages musicals, *Jungle Book* and *The Little Princess* to name two, in which all performers are children (aged 6 to 18) who are students in their after-school theater arts programs and summer camps. Christian Youth Theater performances are generally held at Lewis Middle School. *Traditions of Christmas* brings CCT and CYT performers together every December for a spectacular holiday revue at Symphony Hall. Tickets for all CCT and CYT shows are very affordable and may just hook the whole family on drama.

SEASONS AND TIMES
➤ CCT: June—Aug, performances on Mt. Helix. Spring auditions. Call for more information. CYT: Classes and performances include fall, winter and spring sessions. Call for current schedule and showtimes.

COST
➤ Show tickets: $6 to $35. Call for CYT tuition information

GETTING THERE
➤ To CCT/CYT headquarters by car, travel Interstate 8 east to Johnson Ave. Exit. Go north on Johnson, then east at Fletcher Parkway. Turn north on Pioneer Way. About 20 minutes from Old Town.

NEARBY
➤ Family Fun Center.

COMMENT
➤ Plays usually run 1 1/2 to 2 hours.

Clown Around at
FERN STREET CIRCUS

Golden Hills Recreation Center
2600 Golf Course Dr., San Diego
(619) 235-1138, (619) 235-9756 (Circus Offices)
www.fernstreetcircus.org

Phenomenal and funny, Fern Street Circus's boldly colorful and kitschy staging and costumes play up the fun and funk of the performers—aged six through adult. You'll see juggling, clowning, acrobatics, stilt walkers, trapeze artists, unicyclists and more. Performers learn and hone their abilities in the After-School Circus Skills Program, a free-of-charge weekly clinic designed for trying all types of clowning ability.

The program is held at the Golden Hills Recreation Center and enthusiastic professionals provide instruction at all levels. Performances (complete with live music) take place all year long throughout San Diego at local parks, community fairs, parades and other sites. Call or check the Fern Street Circus website for current performance information.

Providing brilliant education and entertainment in the circus arts, Fern Street Circus is San Diego's only professional circus, and a cherished member of the community.

SEASONS AND TIMES
➤ After-School Circus Skills Program: Mon and Fri., 4 pm—6 pm.
Performances: Call or visit website for upcoming performances.

COST
➤ After-School Circus Skills Program: Free, registration required.
Performances: $5 to $10.

GETTING THERE
➤ By car, from Interstate 5 south exit at Pershing Dr. Turn east on
26th St. and east again on Golf Course Dr. About 10 minutes from
Old Town. See website for details about performance venues.

COMMENT
➤ Performances last about 1 hour.

All the World's a Stage
OLD GLOBE THEATRE

1363 Old Globe Way, San Diego
(619) 231-1941
www.oldglobe.org

You're guaranteed to have a memorable experience the moment you set foot inside the Old Globe Theatre, which mimics the bard's Globe Playhouse in London. Viewing a Shakespearean play, a contemporary drama or musical is just icing on the cake at this 600-seat theater. Housed in the Simon Edison Center for the Performing Arts, the Old Globe is part of a three theater complex including the Cassius Carter Center Stage and the Lowell Davies Festival Theatre—a unique outdoor stage where you can watch plays under the stars.

World-renowned for its work, the Old Globe puts on over a dozen different plays each year—including the extremely popular *How the Grinch Stole Christmas* from November to December. The Old Globe education department supplies study guides, play guides and teacher workshops, as well as special student matinées and backstage tours by appointment. Call for more information (619-231-1941, ext. 2142). The gift shop sells unique theater-related merchandise and Lady Carolyn's Pub serves up soups, salads, desserts and juice if you get hungry between acts.

SEASONS AND TIMES
➤ Year-round: Call or visit website for current schedule.

COST
➤ Tickets $12 to $45, depending on performance and seat location.

GETTING THERE
➤ By car, from Interstate 5 south exit Sassafras St. Go east at Laurel St., and drive into Balboa Park. Park in area lots. From Hwy. 163 south, Exit Park Blvd. Turn north and go to President's Way. Enter the park heading west and park in area lots. About 10 minutes from Old Town.
➤ By public transit, take bus route 7/7A/7B to Park Blvd. and Village Place. Walk El Prado west to the Old Globe.

NEARBY
➤ Fleet Science Center, San Diego Junior Theatre, Model Railroad Museum, Natural History Museum, Museum of Man, San Diego Museum of Art, Starlight Musical Theatre.

COMMENT
➤ Plays usually run 1 ½ to 2 hours with an intermission.

Sugar Plum Fairies at the
CITY BALLET
OF SAN DIEGO

Spreckels Theatre
121 Broadway, San Diego
(858) 272-8663, (858) 274-6058 (Ballet Offices)
www.cityballet.org

See children's eyes sparkle as they experience their first shimmering ballet. With any luck, it'll be the seasonal performance of *The Nutcracker*, held in historic Spreckels Theatre. The sets and costumes are elaborate and glittery—just the way aspiring swans and fairies like them. And don't miss the Sugar Plum Fairy Party, just for kids prior to special *Nutcracker* showings, with snacks, magical fairies and up-close opportunities with performers.

Performing concerts throughout the year at varying venues, the City Ballet succeeds in producing high-quality shows that appeal to all ages. In addition to their annual schedule (highlighted by *Nutcracker* performances in December and the Spring Concert performed with the San Diego Civic Youth Orchestra), the Ballet strives to provide outreach programs and educational ventures, including their Discover a Dancer program, which offers dance training for disadvantaged children. City Ballet incorporates live music whenever possible, enhancing every leap, pirouette and plié. Call for current performance schedule and prices.

SEASONS AND TIMES
➤ Year-round. Call or visit website for current performance schedule.

COST
➤ Tickets $12 to $39.

GETTING THERE
➤ By car to Spreckels Theatre, travel Interstate 5 south to Front St. Turn east and seek street parking. About 10 minutes from Old Town.
➤ By public transit, take the Blue Line trolley to Civic Center Trolley Station. Walk southwest to Broadway.

SIMILAR ATTRACTIONS
➤ California Ballet Company, 8276 Ronson Rd., San Diego (858) 560-5676. San Diego Ballet, 5304 Metro St., San Diego (619) 294-7378.

COMMENT
➤ Plan a 2-hour visit.

What's My Line?
SAN DIEGO
JUNIOR THEATRE

Casa Del Prado Theatre
in Balboa Park, San Diego
(619) 239-1311
www.juniortheatre.com

Achieving its 54th season in 2002, San Diego Junior Theatre is the oldest continuing children's theater program in the country. Putting on six shows a year in the picturesque Casa del Prado Theatre in historic Balboa Park (page 15), the cast and crew of Junior Theatre productions are students in Junior Theatre programs and range in age from 8 to 18.

Junior Theatre offers acting, singing and dance instruction, as well as summer camps and drama clubs for specific age groups—there's even a newsletter tailored to young thespians. The non-profit organization stages big Broadway musicals, fairy tale favorites, classic Shakespeare and occasionally, local original works. The high-quality performances have ensured Junior Theatre's longevity —with illustrious alumni such as Raquel Welch and Dennis Hopper. Tickets are inexpensive, so season subscriptions for families are affordable. With professional directors and designers, strong community support and a mission to encourage children's creativity, self-esteem and enjoyment of theater arts, Junior Theatre is an exceptional experience— whether your kids choose to be in the audience, on the stage, or behind the scenes.

SEASONS AND TIMES
➤ Year-round. Call for current performance schedule or class information.

COST
➤ Adults and children $5 to $9, depending on seat location. Call for current pricing of classes and camps.

GETTING THERE

➤ By car, from Hwy. 163 south, exit Park Blvd. Head north, then turn west at Village Place into Balboa Park. Limited area parking. About 10 minutes from Old Town.

➤ By public transit, take bus route 7/7A/7B to Park Blvd. and Village Place. Walk west to Casa del Prado Theatre.

NEARBY

➤ San Diego Museum of Art, Fleet Science Center, Natural History Museum, Model Railroad Museum, Old Globe Theatre, Museum of Man, Starlight Musical Theatre.

COMMENT

➤ Diaper-changing facilities available. Limited immediate parking.

Strings and Things
SAN DIEGO SYMPHONY

Copley Symphony Hall
750 B St., San Diego
(619) 231-0938 or (619) 235-0800
www.sandiegosymphony.com

The power and beauty of music is brought to life right before your eyes at the Copley Symphony Hall. For tykes who take music lessons, sing in a choir or enjoy the rattling of pots and pans, taking a trip to see the San Diego Symphony is a delightful adventure.

The season, which runs from October to May, serves up 42 concerts plus a horde of other family-friendly entertainment options. The symphony holds special holiday concerts, educational and other outreach programs. Kids Concerts build an appreciation of music with interactive educational performances that unite thousands of students and educators. School Sounds reaches out to all grade levels, customizing programs that may include musician visits to the classroom. In summer, Summer Pops is a ten-week series held outdoors at Navy Pier where families can enjoy whiling away an afternoon.

Visit the Symphony website or call for a current concert calendar and information on some other happenings. Season subscriptions available.

SEASONS AND TIMES
➤ Year-round. Call for current schedule.

COST
➤ Generally $15 to $59, call for details.

GETTING THERE
➤ By car, from Hwy. 163 south, exit B St. Follow B St. west across 12th St./Park Blvd. to Symphony Hall. About 10 minutes from Old Town.
➤ By public transit, ride bus route 34 to stop at 9th Ave. and C St. Walk northwest to B St.

NEARBY
➤ Balboa Park, Coronado, Gaslamp Quarter, Seaport Village.

COMMENT
➤ Plan a 2-hour visit.

On the Silver Screen
SPECIAL CINEMA

Oftentimes we forget that going to a theater used to be the only way to catch a flick. Treat the kids (and yourself) and head out to the nearest theater to watch something on the big screen. Munch on buttery popcorn and soak up movie theater atmosphere—or experience one of the more unusual options listed below. After all, in San Diego you can watch a movie on a mainsail, at a park, on a huge IMAX™ or OMNIMAX™ screen or at a drive-in. Enjoy!

MARITIME MUSEUM
1306 N. Harbor Dr., San Diego
(619) 234-9153
www.sdmaritime.com
An annual summer film festival put on by the Maritime Museum. Families hop aboard the *Star of India* to see Swiss Family Robinson, Treasure Island and other such classics shown upon the glorious ship's mainsail.

SAN DIEGO PARK AND RECREATION DEPARTMENT
Varying Locations, San Diego
(619) 525-8219
Free family films are offered under the stars at area parks and pools June through August.

FLEET SCIENCE CENTER SPACE THEATER
1875 El Prado in Balboa Park, San Diego
(619) 238-1233
www.rhfleet.org
Presents educational IMAX™ and OMNIMAX™ films on a giant, tilted dome seven stories high. You'll feel you're submerging under the sea to meet dolphins, or sitting atop a giant redwood. Planetarium shows, too.

NATURAL HISTORY MUSEUM
CHARMAINE AND MAURICE KAPLAN THEATER
1788 El Prado in Balboa Park, San Diego
(619) 232-3821
www.sdnhm.org
Shows large-format film in this state-of-the-art theater opened in
2001, with themes pertaining to accompanying Museum exhibits as
well as ecology, wildlife and other natural history topics.

Drive-In Movie Theaters

AERO DRIVE-IN
1470 E. Broadway, El Cajon
(619) 444-8800

SANTEE DRIVE-IN
10990 Woodside Ave., Santee
(619) 448-7447

SOUTH BAY DRIVE-IN
2170 Coronado, Imperial Beach
(619) 423-2727

VALLEY DRIVE-IN
3480 Mission Ave., Oceanside
(760) 757-5556

I Wish I May, I Wish I Might...
STARLIGHT MUSICAL THEATRE

2005 Pan American Plaza, San Diego
(619) 544-7827
www.starlighttheatre.org

There is indeed something magical about singing, dancing and storytelling beneath the stars. At Starlight Bowl, the Balboa Park outdoor venue where Starlight Theatre presents a glorious summer season, it's even more special.

Starlight is the ideal introductory theater experience for kids. Child-familiar shows such as *Peter Pan* and *Wizard of Oz* are among the three musical productions staged each June through September. Join in the tradition of pre-show picnics on the lawn areas surrounding the Bowl.

Watch for the mysterious red box that appears on stage during every performance. It's a sewing box that was once left on stage accidentally, and is now believed to bring good luck. Also amusing is the actors' ability to "freeze" when planes fly over—be amazed as they flawlessly resume dialogue when the skies quiet. For families seeking a bargain, Thursday and Sunday performances are free for children under 13.

SEASONS AND TIMES
➤ June—Sept, curtain time 8 pm. Box office opens in Mar.

COST
➤ Tickets $9 to $39.50, depending on seat location. Under 13 free on Thu and Sun.

GETTING THERE
➤ By car, from Hwy. 163 south, exit Park Blvd. Turn north, then west at Presidents Way. At the stop sign continue west, then follow the one-way loop south. Free parking. Starlight Bowl located immediately east of Aerospace Museum. About 10 minutes from Old Town.
➤ By public transit, take bus route 7/7A/7B to President's Way. Walk west to stop sign, then south toward Starlight Bowl.

NEARBY
➤ Fleet Science Center, San Diego Junior Theatre, Model Railroad Museum, Museum of Man, Natural History Museum, Old Globe Theatre, San Diego Museum of Art.

COMMENT
➤ No strollers. Wheelchairs by arrangement.

OTHER MUSIC, THEATER, DANCE & CINEMA

CLASSICS FOR KIDS
(619) 435-9111
www.classics4kids.org
Striving to create new audiences for classical music, this group produces theatrical works introducing the genre in a playful way.

FREE SUMMER CONCERTS
(619) 525-8129
www.sannet.gov
Many park and recreation facilities throughout San Diego hold free concerts in the summer. Call your neighborhood recreation center to find out more, or use the contact information above to find complete listing.

LAMB'S PLAYERS THEATRE
(619) 437-6050
www.lambsplayers.org
This long-established group is based in Coronado and provides
family-friendly theatrical performances.

MARIE HITCHCOCK PUPPET THEATRE
(619) 685-5045
Located in the Palisades area of Balboa Park, this theater brings in
puppeteers from all over to perform Wed–Sun.

SAN DIEGO CHILDREN'S CHOIR
(760) 632-5467
www.sdcchoir.org
Instruction, rehearsal and performance for youths (8 to 18). Low
cost tuition, scholarships available.

SAN DIEGO CIVIC YOUTH BALLET
(619) 233-3060
www.sdcyb.org
A San Diego institution providing instruction and performance.

SAN DIEGO OPERA
(619) 231-6915
www.sdopera.com
Performs major operas at Civic Center and presents special
concerts and outreach programs throughout the city.

SAN DIEGO SCHOOL OF
CREATIVE AND PERFORMING ARTS
(619) 470-0555
www.scpa.snadi.net
A school for 6th to 12th grade students. Offers instruction in all
aspects of performing and creative arts within a 40-acre complex.

SAN DIEGO YOUTH SYMPHONY
(619) 233-3232
www.sdys.org
A respected orchestral training program for all levels. Performances
throughout the year.

CHAPTER 6

ANIMALS, FARMS, AND ZOOS

Introduction

In San Diego, getting close to plants and animals that share our planet can mean such exciting activities as petting a stingray at the Chula Vista Nature Center or attending a Critter Camp at Helen Woodward Animal Center. The varied locations in this chapter offer personal encounters with animals of all types, and enticing outdoor explorations from tidepools to traditional farms.

Ride a hay wagon at Bell Gardens or watch frolicking seals at the Children's Pool. Visit a flock of talking birds at the Aviary and then sign up for a horseback ride at any one of the places listed under Places to Ride. For a scrumptious afternoon activity, pick strawberries and enjoy fresh fruit off the vine. Best of all, your family will have a chance to take in the day at a less frantic pace. Picnic lunches and casual attire are encouraged for all activities in this chapter.

Bountiful Harvest
BELL GARDENS

**30841 Cole Grade Rd., Valley Center
(760) 749-6297
www.bellgardensfarm.com**

Want to take in blue skies, rolling hills and fields bursting with all kinds of fresh produce? Spend a day at beautiful Bell Gardens and your kids will learn what country living is all about.

While the farm's produce market (serving up berries, squash, corn, tomatoes and plenty more) is a big draw, don't neglect the rest of this 115-acre working farm. Founded by Mr. Glen Bell, Jr. of Taco Bell™ fame, the farm boasts spacious lawns, shady trees, walking trails and picnic tables for your family's enjoyment.

For the younger set, Ghost Canyon is a treat with its easy hiking trail haunted by bed sheet ghosts and peering, painted eyes. There's a cornstalk maze to navigate and geese to meet. Keep a sharp lookout for Taco, the cat. Pay three dollars per person and ride on a tractor-tugged hay wagon and aboard an open-air quarter-scale train. Whimsical scarecrows will greet you throughout your adventure as you chug past human-made waterfalls, a trestle bridge, Bell Junction and Kathleen Lake (complete with ducks).

On weekends, tours run every half-hour, no reservations required. Call ahead on weekdays to see if there's a tour scheduled. Groups are welcome (call ahead).Educational field trips include a fresh-grown snack and hands-on picking opportunities.

SEASONS AND TIMES
➤ Apr—Oct: Daily, 10 am—6 pm. Nov—Mar: Daily, 10 am—4 pm. Closed Thanksgiving, Christmas and rainy days.

COST
➤ Free. Hay wagon farm tours and train ride: Adults and children $3.

GETTING THERE
➤ By car, take Hwy. 163 north to Interstate 15 north. Exit Via Rancho Pkwy. and turn east. Follow the road (it will turn into Bear Valley Pkwy.) until it ends at Valley Pkwy., then turn east. Follow the road through town (it will turn into Valley Center Rd.) until the traffic signal at Cole Grade Rd. Turn north and drive 3 miles to entrance. About 55 minutes from Old Town.

COMMENT
➤ Plan a 2-hour visit.

See Smiling Seals at
CHILDREN'S POOL

Coast Blvd., La Jolla
(619) 221-8900

The Children's Pool was once a place for kids to frolic. Its shallow beach and protective sea wall made it an ideal swimming location. Today however, you won't see any youngsters swimming here—at least not of the human variety.

The pool is now home to California seals and sea lions, which swim about, lounge on rocks and roll right up on the sand to catch a few rays. There's an extended sidewalk alongside the pool, which provides excellent views of these adorable creatures without disturbing them. Explain to your kids that these seals are wild animals and considered protected wildlife, so people aren't allowed to feed them or get too close.

Once you're finished viewing, take a short walk north to La Jolla Cove where you can enter Sunny Jim Cave and descend 145 steps (some dark and slippery) to view crashing blue waves through this giant grotto. Keep a look out for more wildlife. You're likely to see pelicans, dolphins, fish and other marine mammals. Enter the Cave through the Cave Store (858-459-0746), which also sells coffee and gifts.

SEASONS AND TIMES
➤ Year-round: Daily, dawn—dusk. Cave Store: Daily, 9 am—dusk.

COST
➤ Children's Pool: Free. Cave Walk: $2.

GETTING THERE
➤ By car, from Interstate 5 north and exit at Ardath Rd. Travel to Prospect St., turning west to Coast Blvd. Street parking is difficult on weekends. About 15 minutes from Old Town.
➤ By public transit, board bus route 5 and travel to University Town Center. Transfer to bus route 34 and get off at Torrey Pines Rd. and Prospect St. Walk north toward Coast Blvd.
➤ By bike, pedal north out of Mission or Pacific Beach along Mission Blvd., which turns into La Jolla Blvd., then Prospect St. Follow Jenner St. down to Coast Blvd.

NEARBY
➤ Birch Aquarium at Scripps, Torrey Pines State Reserve.

COMMENT
➤ Plan a 2-hour visit. Limited stroller/wheelchair access in Children's Pool area.

Get Close to Nature at
CHULA VISTA
NATURE CENTER

1000 Gunpowder Point Dr., Chula Vista
(619) 409-5900
www.chulavistanaturecenter.org

Board a free shuttle from the parking lot at the Sweetwater Marsh National Wildlife Refuge and ride it to the Chula Vista Nature Center. Here you'll learn about the wildlife that lives within the 316-acre preserve. From 200 species of bird to ocean creatures, the Nature Center provides an excellent opportunity to meet and learn about the Refuge's many animal inhabitants.

Live species are part of the exhibits, including interactive displays that invite kids to crawl up and peek at a "house mouse" or under a tank to see a crab's eye view of a stingray. There are also sea horses, snakes, toads and moon jellies to look at. Outside, visit the petting pool where you can safely stroke horn and leopard sharks, bat and stingrays, as well as a funny looking (but very friendly) shovel-nosed guitarfish. Children need to be instructed to wash their hands first and to treat the creatures gently.

Say hello to Verdi, the green iguana who enjoys the sunshine upon the patio. Don't miss the burrowing owl habitat and the clapper rail trail and aviary. Two observation decks make for great bird watching—bring your binoculars or rent a pair from the bookstore. Once you've seen enough, strike out from the Center toward the San Diego Bay shoreline on one of the easy walking trails.

On the weekend, there are craft workshops for only 50 cents. Special events include bird walks, bug walks and behind-the-scenes tours. The Nature Center also offers unique environmental-themed birthday parties. Group tours must schedule in advance.

SEASONS AND TIMES
➤ Sept—May: Tue—Sun, 10 am—5 pm. June—Aug: Mon—Sun, 10 am—5 pm. Closed Thanksgiving, Christmas Eve, Christmas Day, New Year's Eve, New Year's and Easter Sunday. Subject to change, call for confirmation.

COST
➤ Adults $3.50, seniors (over 64) $2.50, youth (6 to 17) $1, under 6 free. Cash only.

GETTING THERE
➤ By car, travel Interstate 5 south to the E St. Exit. Turn west into the parking lot. Shuttles run every 20 minutes to take guests to the Center from the parking lot. Free parking. About a 20-minute drive from Old Town.
➤ By public transit, ride the Blue Line trolley to the Bayfront/E St. Trolley Station. Walk west to the Nature Center parking lot..

NEARBY
➤ Knott's Soak City.

COMMENT
➤ Plan a 1 1/2-hour visit. Diaper-changing facilities available.

Brilliant Birds
FREE FLIGHT AVIARY

2132 Jimmy Durante Blvd., Del Mar
(858) 481-3148

Just listen for the squawks, twitters and bird-song as you drive by and you can't miss Del Mar's Free Flight Aviary. This compact tropical paradise houses parrots, cockatoos, macaws and more. Families are welcome to enter this outdoor garden created for feathered beauties, to gain an up-close appreciation of these brilliantly colored birds.

When you arrive, ask a staff member to explain the brief do's and don'ts of touching and handling the birds. They'll first ask you to wash your hands, then you're free to stroll about and meet the residents. A chorus of welcoming "hellos," ring out from the most talkative creatures, sitting on their perches under a canopy of shady trees. Some of the friendliest fellows lean in, beg for your hand and a seat on your shoulder, while others are content to let you watch them eat, snapping and cracking at their seeds. The "biters" are roped off and not for touching, but easy to view. The facility is adjacent to a veterinary business and offers bird supplies and sales, as well as bird boarding. Call ahead if you're interested in bringing in a group.

SEASONS AND TIMES
➣ Year-round: Daily, 10 am–5 pm. Closed rainy days and major holidays.

COST
➣ Admission $1.

GETTING THERE
➣ By car, from Interstate 5 north, exit Via de la Valle and turn west. At Jimmy Durante Blvd. turn south. Located on west side, just past Del Mar Fairgrounds. Free parking. About 25 minutes from Old Town.
➣ By bike, ride north on Hwy. 101 just past Village of Del Mar. Located on west side.

NEARBY
➣ Del Mar Fairgrounds.

COMMENT
➣ Plan a 45-minute visit.

Cold Nose, Warm Heart
HELEN WOODWARD ANIMAL CENTER

6461 El Apajo Rd., Rancho Santa Fe
(858) 756-4117
www.animalcenter.org

No matter how many cold noses and wagging tails might be running around the place, once you step inside you know it's filled with warm hearts. The Helen Woodward Animal Center is a neatly run 12-acre facility in the affluent community of Rancho Santa Fe. It houses adoption kennels for dogs and other pets, a boarding facility, classrooms, a veterinary hospital, horse stables and an arena for the Center's Therapeutic Riding Program—tailored specifically for those with physical disabilities.

The center runs public awareness and educational programs throughout the year. Spring and summer sessions of Critter Camp allow 4- to 13-year-olds the opportunity to get friendly with a variety of creatures, from snakes to sheep and hamsters to horses. There's also the Animal Lover's Club (for ages five to ten) that meets twice monthly to learn and care for the Center's four-legged friends. In addition to field trips, assembly, and Scout badge programs, the education department also offers specialized playgroup visits, and First Friends—a parent and tot program offering positive experiences with animals. The supervised birthday parties include crafts, games and pet visits. The Center offers free tours and animal visits one weekend each month. Call ahead for information and reservations.

SEASONS AND TIMES
➤ Year-round: Call for program and tour times.

COST
➤ Call for individual program fees.

GETTING THERE
➤ By car, from Interstate 5 north, exit Via de la Valle and turn east. Travel to El Apajo, turn south. Follow to entrance. Free parking. About 40 minutes from Old Town.

COMMENT
➤ For tours, plan a 1-hour visit.

SIMILAR ATTRACTION
➤ San Diego Humane Society. 887 Sherman St., San Diego, (619) 299-7012. www.sdhumane.org

U-Pick
PLACES TO PICK FRESH PRODUCE

No matter what the season, families can find a farm with something wonderful for the picking. Let your kids enjoy the satisfaction of selecting fresh berries straight from the field, plucking the plumpest orange pumpkin off the vine or digging up their own poinsettia to take home.

BATES NUT FARM
15954 Woods Valley Rd., Valley Center
(760) 749-3333
In addition to nuts, the farm offers u-pick pumpkins and Christmas trees seasonally. There's a gourmet food store, gift shop, picnic tables, goats, sheep, ducks and geese to see. Inquire about special events.

LESLIE FARMS
Cannon Rd. near Legoland Dr., Carlsbad
(760) 438-5071
Gather up the whole clan and pick your own peck of luscious strawberries. Open May— August. Call ahead for school group discounts.

WEIDNER'S GARDENS
695 Normandy Rd., Encinitas
(760) 436-2194
These family-owned gardens provide wheelbarrows and whatever else you'll need to get grubby and grow your own flower garden Remember to bring carrots for the miniature horses.

PINERY PUMPKIN PATCHES
5437 Bonita Rd., Bonita
13421 Highland Valley Rd., Escondido
(858) 566-7466
The patches open Oct 1 for pumpkin picking. There are farm
animals to pet, cornstalk mazes to explore and hay wagons to ride.

FAMILY CHRISTMAS TREE FARM
300 Pepper Dr., El Cajon
(619) 448-5331
Choose and cut your own pine tree. Tools provided. Open seasonally.

PINERY TREE FARM
5437 Bonita Rd., Bonita
(619) 475-8733
Choose and cut your own tree. Thanksgiving through Christmas Eve.

Giddy-Up!
PLACES TO RIDE

L asso your little buckaroos and play cowboy
for a while at these excellent equestrian
locales. Rates start around $25 an hour per
person for guided trail rides. Whether your family
hankers for a ride along a scenic mountaintop or a
beach at sunset, both are possibilities in San
Diego. Most stables require riders to be at least
seven years old.

BRIGHT VALLEY FARMS
12310 Campo Rd., Spring Valley
(619) 670-1861
Offers guided trail rides, as well as horseback riding lessons.

HAPPY TRAILS HORSE RENTAL
12115 Black Mountain Rd., San Diego
(858) 271-8777
Enter the wild west feel of this facility, complete with barnyard
animals, stagecoach rides and guided trail rides.

SANDY'S RENTAL STABLE
2060 Hollister St., San Diego
(619) 424-3124
www.sandysrentalstable.com
Located adjacent to the Tijuana Estuary State Park and Preserve, saddle up for beach and trail rides. Chuck wagon meal rides, group arrangements and gift certificates available.

SWEETWATER FARMS
3051 Equitation Lane, Bonita
(619) 475-3134
www.sweethorses.com
Offering pony rides every weekend, horseback riding lessons for age six and up, day camps and birthday parties.

Visit Tiny Creatures at
TIDEPOOLS

Youngsters enjoy small things, so be sure to schedule a visit to a tidepool and examine the tiny, fascinating creatures that call these natural rock formations home. Along the shoreline, there are plenty of nooks, crannies and craters for the varied sea and plant life. Plan to visit tidepools at low tide—otherwise they simply vanish under the surf. Check the newspaper or call (619) 221-8824 for low tide times. Then throw on some old clothes and shoes you don't mind getting wet and head for the water.

Before you arrive, advise children to move slowly, look carefully and not to touch the fragile habitats. Crabs, anemones and mussels are just a few examples of sea life you'll find dwelling in San Diego tidepools. Here's a sampling of San Diego's best (and most accessible) tidepools.

CABRILLO NATIONAL MONUMENT (PAGE 137)

Travel Interstate 8 west to Sunset Cliffs Blvd., then southeast onto to Nimitz St. Turn south on Catalina St. toward Cabrillo National Monument. Turn west on the roadway just before the entry kiosk. The Cabrillo Monument Visitor Center offers free handouts to guide your tidepool trip.

LA JOLLA

Travel Interstate 5 north to Ardath Rd. Turn north on La Jolla Shores, then west on Avenida de La Playa. Park at the Shores or surrounding area, and walk south down the beach.

OCEAN BEACH

Drive Interstate 8 west to Sunset Cliffs Blvd. Follow Sunset Cliffs to Newport Ave., turn west. Park in lot to the south, next to the Pier.

"TABLETOPS" AT CARDIFF

Drive Interstate 5 north to Birmingham Dr. west. Head south on Highway 101, and park before you reach Solana Beach.

OTHER ANIMALS, FARMS AND ZOOS

MONARCH BUTTERFLY PROGRAM

450 Ocean View Ave., Encinitas
(760) 944-7113
A butterfly house with several species and the opportunity to learn about the metamorphasis from caterpillar, chrysalis to beloved butterfly.
Open May–Oct.

WILLIAMS WORM FARM

14893 El Monte Rd., Lakeside
(619) 443-1698
A working worm ranch where kids can get an educational tour.

CHAPTER 7

GREEN SPACES

Introduction

Aah....a breath of fresh air. There's nothing better than spending a beautiful sunny day outside. And what more enjoyable way for your family to spend time outdoors than by hiking, wildlife watching or having a picnic at one of San Diego's green spaces.

The green spaces are entwined throughout the county in startling variety. Beyond its many city parks teeming with trim lawns and jungle gyms, San Diego keeps a cache of unique, nature-loving locales. In this chapter you'll discover rugged trails to conquer within Mission Trails Regional Park— accompanied by the opportunity to visit its superb Visitor and Interpretive Center. At Quail Botanical Gardens, stroll through one of the rarest plant collections in the world. And if you're not sailing or skiing upon the waters of Mission Bay Park, then surely you'll be tempted by its acres of green lawns that stretch to the shore, perfect for kite flying.

Pedal Power
LAKE POWAY

Lake Poway Rd., Poway
(858) 679-4393
www.ci.poway.ca.us/lakepowa.html

Lake Poway Park has two playgrounds, sand volleyball courts, ball fields and rolling grass-covered slopes complete with picnic tables, barbecues, and pavilions. It's a pleasant green space all on its own, but snuggled up to Lake Poway, it promises a full day of outdoor adventure.

One of the best ways to explore Lake Poway's 60 acres is by paddle boat. Rent one of these little blue wonders and kick up the pedal power. You can cruise the lake, visit the shorelines and say hello to resident ducks and geese. Canoes and rowboats are also available for rent, as are fishing gear and permits. Tote along some bird feed for the friendly waterfowl.

For more fun, Lake Poway Trail is a 2.7-mile loop affording pleasing views of the lake and Mount Woodson beyond. Horses and leashed dogs are allowed on the trail, and because it's rugged terrain for kids under ten to hike, think about riding your mountain bikes. Trail user guides are available at the concession stand (open Wednesday through Sunday).

Lake Poway hosts family camp-outs, fishing derbies and a summer day camp. Less than a mile away (you can hike or drive), the spectacular Blue Sky Ecological Reserve maintains trails, interpretive signage and outstanding ranger programs such as family campfires, stargazing and Owl Prowls. Many animals call Blue Sky home—among them bobcats, bullfrogs, coyotes and cottontails. For more information on the reserve, visit http://users.abac.com/bluesky or call (858) 679-5469.

SEASONS AND TIMES
➤ Park: Year-round, daily, dawn—dusk. Lake: Wed—Sun, 7 am—dusk.

COST
➤ Apr—Oct: $4 per vehicle on weekends and holidays (for non-residents of Poway). Other months free. Call for boat rental and fishing permit prices.

GETTING THERE
➤ By car, from Interstate 15 north, exit on Rancho Bernardo Rd., heading east. Travel approximately 4 miles (it turns into Espola Rd.), then turn east on Lake Poway Rd. About 40 minutes from Old Town.

NEARBY
➤ Old Poway Park.

COMMENT
➤ Plan a 3-hour visit. In-line skates and skateboards are not permitted at the park. Trails not wheelchair/stroller accessible.

Take a Hike
LOS PENASQUITOS CANYON PRESERVE

Black Mountain Rd. and Mercy Rd., San Diego
(858) 484-3219 or (858) 538-8066

I f you've got little hikers (or hope to develop some), plan a trek through Los Penasquitos Canyon Preserve. Most trails are easily managed and the varied vegetation covering the canyons is lovely. Perennial streams run throughout and if your family is up for a six-mile round trip, you can visit a waterfall tumbling from stately boulders. While there are no tables, there are places to picnic just off the beaten path. Eucalyptus, sycamore, and oak trees abound, and in spring wildflowers will decorate your journey. Leashed dogs are allowed, mountain bikes are permitted on the fire roads and you'll likely encounter a few visitors on horseback, too.

For a historic highlight, visit on the weekend and enjoy the Adobe Ranch Tour (phone ahead for tour times). Built in the 1800s, the property is part of the first Mexican land grant in California—an area ranched for over a 100 years. Interpretive walks and other programs are offered throughout the year. There are no restrooms or piped water—so bring plenty of drinking water along. Canyonside Park borders the reserve to the north and has a playground, restrooms, ball fields and other traditional city park amenities.

SEASONS AND TIMES
➦ Year-round: Daily, 8 am—dusk. Call for Adobe Ranch Tour and special program times.

COST
➦ Free.

GETTING THERE
➦ By car, travel Interstate 15 north to Mercy Rd. Exit west, follow to Black Mountain Rd. Proceed west into parking lot. For Adobe Ranch parking lot, turn north on Black Mountain Rd, west into Canyonside Park driveway. About 25 minutes from Old Town.

COMMENT
➦ Plan a 3-hour visit. Trails are not wheelchair/stroller accessible.

Swim Like Fish
MISSION BAY PARK

East Mission Bay Dr., San Diego
(619) 221-8900 or (619) 276-2071 (Visitor Center)
www.aboutmissionbay.com

If your kids swim like fish, this is the place for your family. Mission Bay Park serves up nearly 2,500 acres of watery wonderland, perfect for boating, jet-skiing, water-skiing, sailing and other water sports. In summer, there are eight supervised swimming sites, but ensure you read all the signs about water quality before diving in. At the Hilton Resort (619-276-4010) you'll find water sport, skate and bike rentals in addition to refreshments.

For those not-so-aquatically inclined, Mission Bay has another 2,500 acres of playgrounds, paved trails, expansive green lawns and shady palms. Any day of the week you'll encounter families flying kites, kids on scooters, tykes with training wheels and in-line skating parents pushing strollers. The smooth, flat paths are perfect for cruising. Along the way, enjoy watching waterfowl, shell collecting, or a barbecue. Take in a game on the volleyball or basketball courts, or watch a round of horseshoes at the north end of the park.

There are plenty of play areas here, but none better than Tecolote Shores with its pretend pirate ship, spider web and other fun structures. Best of all, it is situated next to the natural sandbox and gentle waters of Mission Bay. If you need more details about the park, check out the Visitor Information Center just off Interstate 5 at the Clairemont Drive Exit. The center offers information on recreation at the Bay, as well as resources for a San Diego stay including hotel, restaurant information and discounted tickets to various attractions. Contact Campland on the Bay (858-581-4200) for camping information and reservations.

SEASONS AND TIMES
➤ Year-round: Daily, dawn—2 am.

COST
➤ Free.

GETTING THERE
➤ By car, from Interstate 5 north exit SeaWorld Dr. heading west. Follow signs for another quick turn west onto East Mission Bay Dr. About 10 minutes from Old Town.
➤ By public transit, take bus route 5A to stop at Fourth and

Broadway. Transfer to bus route 50 and get off at Clairemont Dr. and Denver St. Walk west toward Mission Bay Park and Visitor Center.

NEARBY
➤ Presidio Park, SeaWorld.

COMMENT
➤ Plan a 3-hour visit.

Get Back to Nature at
MISSION TRAILS
REGIONAL PARK

1 Father Junipero Serra Trail, San Diego
(619) 668-3275
www.mtrp.org

To get the most from this 5800-acre park, start at the Visitor Center located at the address above. You will learn about the area's history and wildlife, as well as the park's recreational opportunities. Also check out the schedule of guided nature walks and other programs offered.

On your way into the center, read about the creatures that inhabit the local landscape—and hear their various calls and sounds. The outdoor amphitheater is graced with sculpted visitors, such as a coyote and a mountain lion who are permanently posing for pictures. Inside, you'll find displays, interactive exhibits, video presentations and a library. Go upstairs—children love the dim tunnel that hoots and howls, simulating the park at night.

Among the 50 miles of trails within this natural retreat are several easy routes that loop the center, including one that will take you to a babbling brook and past grinding stones created by the Kumeyaay Native Americans. Nearby is historic Mission Dam, where water was stored for the early residents of Mission de Alcala. Mountain bikes and leashed dogs are welcome on the trails.

Kumeyaay Lake Campground is a tranquil spot for family camping, and Lake Murray offers boating and fishing (rentals available). A paved trail borders the human-made lake, making it popular for bicycling and in-line skating. There are also picnic tables, playground equipment and ball fields.

SEASONS AND TIMES
➤ Year-round: Daily, 8 am—5 pm, with extended summer hours.

COST
➤ Free.

GETTING THERE
➤ By car, from Hwy. 163 or Interstate 5, take Interstate 8 east. Exit at Mission Gorge Rd. and turn north. Travel approximately 4 miles to marked entrance at Junipero Serra Trail, just past Jackson Dr. About 20 minutes from Old Town.

COMMENT
➤ Plan a 2-hour visit. Visitor Center is completely wheelchair and stroller accessible, as is one paved trail. Diaper-changing facilities available.

Steep Hills and Serra History
PRESIDIO PARK

2811 Jackson St., San Diego
(619) 692-4918

These are the kind of hills made for rolling down. So don't be shy, join in with the kids as they tumble over and over. Just be sure you can stop because the lawns of Presidio Park have some steep slopes, while statuesque trees provide shade and climbing opportunities. Trails take you past historical markers, unusual plants, little bridges and beautiful lookouts. Pack a lunch and make a relaxing day of your trip.

Presidio Park is named for the Royal Presidio, which served as headquarters for Spanish soldiers from 1769 until the 1800s. The spot was actually the original site of the first Mission, where the friars relocated shortly afterwards to make farming easier and to be closer to the Native Americans they sought to convert to Christianity. Now the majestic Presidio houses the Junipero Serra Museum (619-297-3258) with displays and artifacts (including exquisite period furniture and clothing) outlining what life was like long before the turn of the 20th century. Climb the museum tower for stunning views of San Diego—and see photographs that illustrate how the surrounding landscape has changed over the decades.

SEASONS AND TIMES

➤ Park: Year-round, daily, 6 am—10 pm. Museum: Tue—Sun, 10 am—4 pm.

COST

➤ Park: Free. Museum: Adults $5, children (6 to 17) $2, under 6 free.

GETTING THERE

➤ By car, travel Taylor St.(off Interstate 5 or 8) north and turn east on Presidio Dr. About 3 minutes from Old Town.

NEARBY

➤ Mission Bay Park, Old Town, SolidRock Gym, UltraZone.

COMMENT

➤ Plan a 2-hour visit. Park trails not accessible by stroller or wheelchair.

Tropical Treasure
QUAIL BOTANICAL GARDENS

230 Quail Gardens Dr., Encinitas
(760) 436-3036
www.qbgardens.com

Your kids have likely heard of endangered animals—but endangered plants? Located just off the freeway, Quail Botanical Gardens is an exotic treasure tucked between businesses and housing developments. Unknown even to many locals, the Quail Gardens flourish on thirty acres, maintaining one of the most diverse collections of plants in the world—while protecting and teaching others about several species of endangered plants.

Explore the tropical rain forest exhibit, stroll among California native plants, bamboo species and palm varieties, as well as plants from Africa, Himalayas, the Middle East, Australia and more. Wind along the hilly and flat trails laced throughout the gardens (some are not paved). Stop and see the Kumeyaay home site exhibit, which paints a picture of local Native American life. There's also wildlife watching at Overlook Pavilion above a natural coastal sage scrub habitat.

Quail Botanical Gardens maintains a research botanical library on site as well as a nursery and gift shop. The lawn and gazebo are popular for weddings, but your family can claim the space for a picnic. The Gardens offer regular workshops on topics such as composting and basket weaving, in addition to special lectures and summer concerts. Tours take place every Saturday at 10 am and special children's tours are held on the first Tuesday of the month at 10:30 am. Group tours by arrangement.

SEASONS AND TIMES
➤ Year-round: Daily, 9 am—5 pm. Closed Thanksgiving, Christmas and New Year's.

COST
➤ Adults $5, seniors (over 59) $4, children (5 to 12) $2, under 5 free.

GETTING THERE
➤ By car, take Interstate 5 north to Encinitas Blvd., turn east. At Quail Gardens Dr. turn
north. Free parking. About a 20-minute drive from Old Town.
➤ By public transit, take bus route 5 to University Town Center. Then board North County Transit bus 310 to Encinitas Station. Disembark and board 309 and travel to Encinitas Blvd. and West Lake St. stop. Walk north to the Gardens.

COMMENT
➤ Plan a 2-hour visit. Some trails too steep and awkward for
wheelchairs and strollers. Diaper-changing facilities available.

Marshland and Migratory Birds at TIJUANA RIVER ESTUARY

301 Caspian Way, Imperial Beach
(619) 575-3613

Teach your kids about the ruddy duck, surf scoter and sandpiper. No, these aren't the latest slang for radical skateboard tricks, but just a few of the more than 370 species of birds that live or winter within the Tijuana River Estuary. At 2,500 acres, it is the largest wetland preserve on the West Coast and encompasses several ecosystems including salt marshes, mud flats, coastal dunes, coastal sage scrub and river habitats.

Four miles of easy trails guide visitors throughout the Reserve, complete with interpretive signage. Search out and identify the many fragile plants living in this inter-tidal coastal estuary—among them cord grass, pickle weed, shore grass and saltwort. Nature walks are led by rangers every Saturday, but Walker's Guides are available at the Visitor Center if you'd like to strike out on your own. The center is small, but well designed and engaging with interactive exhibits. An excellent Junior Ranger program operates from the center, which also maintains classrooms, audio-visual programs and an education lab. Bring binoculars and quiet voices to experience the best of the reserve—you may spot a golden eagle, a rabbit or a crab during your estuary exploration. Call ahead for group tours and information.

SEASONS AND TIMES
➤ Trails: Year-round, daily, dawn—dusk. Visitor Center: Wed—Sun, 10 am—6 pm (5 pm in winter).

COST
➤ Free.

GETTING THERE
➤ By car, travel Interstate 5 south. Exit west at Coronado Ave. in Imperial Beach. Travel approximately 3 miles. The road will become Imperial Beach Blvd. At Third Ave., turn south. Follow the signs. About 25 minutes from Old Town.

COMMENT
➤ Plan a 2-hour visit. Diaper-changing facilities available.

Boundless Sky
TORREY PINES STATE RESERVE

Coast Hwy. 101, La Jolla
(858) 755-2063

The namesake trees of Torrey Pines State Reserve are over 150 years old and found in only two places on earth; in La Jolla reserve and on Santa Rosa Island, off the coast near Santa

Barbara. You'll enter the Reserve along the water, where families enjoy the sand at Torrey Pines State Beach, but follow the roadway to the upper parking lot for a real appreciation of green spaces.

The Visitor Center should be your first stop. Built of adobe clay bricks, it housed a lodge in the 1920s. Today it introduces visitors to the features of one of the most exceptional collaborations of plants, animals, ocean and sky on earth. The center is filled with many stuffed species—a cougar, pelican, and coyote to name a few, and offers Explore Stations for hands-on learning. You'll find books, teacher guides and gifts, including inexpensive cut-out and origami projects that are educational but feel like a souvenir to the kids. On weekends, there is a ten-minute video presentation offered in addition to guided nature walks at 10 am and 2 pm.

Several trails cut through the reserve, so ask a docent or ranger for a map. One of the best for families is Razor Point Trail, just over a mile round trip, guiding you past wildflowers, deep gorges, fascinating formations and Red Butte that kids love to conquer. At Razor Point, you'll encounter a phenomenal view of the beach and waves. Everyone must stay behind the trail ropes at all times. The area is not only fragile, but the cliffs are extremely unstable. Explain to children that they cannot collect flowers, pine cones, rocks or anything else from within the reserve. They must be left to maintain balance—and breathtaking beauty. Call ahead for group tours.

SEASONS AND TIMES
➤ Year-round: Daily, 8 am—dusk. Visitor Center: 9 am—dusk.

COST

➤ $2 per car.

GETTING THERE

➤ By car, from Interstate 5 north, exit at Carmel Valley Rd. and head west. At Coast Hwy. 101, turn south. Watch for signs and kiosk. Follow the roadway to the upper parking lot to reach Visitor Center and trails. Free parking. About 15 minutes from Old Town.

NEARBY

➤ Birch Aquarium, Children's Pool.

COMMENT

➤ Plan a 2-hour visit. Limited wheelchairs/stroller accessible areas. No food may be brought into the reserve.

OTHER GREEN SPACES

CHOLLAS LAKE PARK

6350 College Grove Dr., San Diego
(619) 527-7683
Free fishing for children on the small lake, easily managed trails among Chollas cacti and eucalyptus trees, a paved walk, playgrounds, picnic tables and barbecues.

CHULA VISTA BAYSIDE PARK

J St. and Marina Pkwy., Chula Vista
(619) 686-6200
Waterfront park with paved walks, play equipment, picnic tables, green lawns, lovely views and nearby boats moored at the marina.

LAKE MIRAMAR

Scripps Lake Dr., San Diego
(619) 465-3474
Features a flat paved trail (nearly five miles) circling the lake. Biking, boat rental, fishing and picnic tables.

MISSION VALLEY RIVER WALK

Mission Center Rd. near Hazard Center Dr., San Diego
(619) 685-1367
A paved trail open for walking, biking or skating.

ROHR PARK
4548 Sweetwater Rd., Chula Vista
(619) 585-5720
This expansive park hosts train rides on 1/8 scale trains one
weekend a month, along with large tree-studded lawns, paved
trails for cycling and in-line skating, as well as playgrounds, picnic
tables and barbecues.

SAN ELIJO LAGOON
2710 Manchester Ave., Encinitas
A refuge of plants, mammals, birds, reptiles and amphibians, the
ecological reserve maintains five miles of trails. An easy one-mile
loop begins at the Nature Center addressed above.

STELZER PARK
11470 Wildcat Canyon Rd., Lakeside
(619) 561-3600
A park designed for enjoyment by disabled children with much of
the play equipment specially designed (others will enjoy as well).
Interpretive center and special ranger programs. Picnic tables,
barbecues, and youth group camping.

TECOLOTE CANYON
Tecolote Rd., San Diego
(858) 581-9952
A small interpretive center marks the trailhead for hiking through
this 970-acre natural park, just east of Mission Bay.

CHAPTER 8

HISTORICAL SITES

Introduction

The secret to San Diego's charm is its history. The city was home to California's first Mission, built by Father Junipero Serra in 1769. The old lighthouse, sitting on the shores of Point Loma since 1855, signaled hundreds of ships in its day. Replete with Maritime history, historical abodes and other fascinating sites, San Diego has been a town of much diversity, rich culture, colorful tales and celebrations long before it had tourist bureaus and overflowing hotels. From the early Native Americans to the Spanish settlers and Portuguese explorers, from the Friars and their missions to the warm influence of neighboring Mexico, a one-of-a-kind blend of cultures and communities has helped create the vibrant, yet mellow feel that *is* San Diego. Uncover San Diego's "secret ingredient" in the following appealing historical sites.

Whales, Trails and Mariner's Tales
CABRILLO NATIONAL MONUMENT

**1800 Cabrillo Memorial Dr., San Diego
(619) 557-5450
www.nps.gov/cabr/**

All year round, there are plenty of educational things to discover at the Cabrillo National Monument. Families enjoy exploring the Cabrillo tidepools (page 115), watching the gray whales swim by on their annual migration, hiking the Bayside Trail or learning about the lighthouse. No matter what the season, this site is a destination must for history-hungry families.

Begin your visit at Old Point Loma Lighthouse, active between 1855 and 1891. It is currently dressed up in furnishings circa 1888. Learn about families who lived and worked in the lighthouse. On special occasions, such as the Cabrillo Festival, visitors can climb to the top of the lighthouse tower for panoramic views. At the Visitor Center, discover the history of Portuguese conquistador Juan Rodriguez Cabrillo, credited with discovering San Diego. Daily slide and film presentations include *Steps to the Sea* (a study of tidepool exploration), *In Search of Cabrillo* (about the explorer's 1542 voyage) and other topics. Ranger-led talks are also offered free each day (call ahead for a schedule). The well-stocked bookstore offers publications ranging from coloring books to research volumes, as well as gifts, educational toys, teacher guides, maps and more.

Bayside Trail is a 2 ½-mile trek with lovely views, but the return trip is steep, unpaved and difficult for young legs. Along the way, see the bunkers and base stations that were situated here during World War I and II and learn about military coastal defense. Other shorter interpretive trails accommodate strollers and wheelchairs. Group tours and educational programs available by arrangement. Snacks and candy available in vending machines.

SEASONS AND TIMES
➤ Year-round: Daily, 9 am—5:15 pm.

COST
➤ $5 per car. Annual passes available.

GETTING THERE
➤ By car, from Interstate 5 heading south or Interstate 8 west, exit at Rosecrans St. At Canon St., turn west. At Catalina Blvd., turn south and follow into the park. Free parking. About 10 minutes from Old Town.
➤ By public transit, take bus route 26 to Cabrillo Monument.

COMMENT
➤ Plan a 2- to 3-hour visit.

Koi and Confucius
CHINESE HISTORICAL MUSEUM

404 Third Ave., San Diego
(619) 338-9888

Housed in a Chinese Mission that has resided in San Diego since 1927, this museum highlights the history of San Diego's Chinatown, which flourished from 1850 to the early 1940s.

You'll discover photographs and dozens of artifacts such as furniture, musical instruments, ornate jade jewelry, hair ornaments, slippers for bound feet and a child's bamboo chair (looking much like an early car seat) from the 1900s. Kids are intrigued with the pieces unearthed during a 1990s excavation of surrounding Chinatown buildings—among them oh-so-familiar marbles, dice and dominoes. Enthusiastic docents enjoy sharing their knowledge and invite children to touch and try some of the artifacts—like the odd-looking wheelbarrow built in the 1800s, but designed nearly 5000 years ago.

Outside, kids enjoy the vibrant color and activity of the koi and goldfish pond and the tiny, tranquil garden with stream and bridge. The research library is available to assist students with projects, and field trips and groups are welcome with advance notice. The Museum hosts a festive Chinese New Year celebration annually and is the cornerstone of the new Asian/Pacific Historic District underway in the vicinity.

SEASONS AND TIMES
➤ Year-round: Tue—Sat, 10:30 am—4 pm; Sun, noon—4 pm.

COST
➤ Free. Donations accepted.

GETTING THERE
➤ By car, from Hwy. 5 heading south, exit at Front St. Drive straight until Market St. then turn east. At Third Ave. turn south. Park in metered street parking. About 10 minutes from Old Town.
➤ By public transit, take the Blue Line trolley to American Plaza Trolley Station. Transfer to the Orange Line and travel to Convention Center Station. Walk east to Third Ave.

NEARBY
➤ Firehouse Museum, Gaslamp Quarter, Maritime Museum, Seaport Village.

COMMENT
➤ Plan a 45-minute visit.

When I Grow Up...
FIREHOUSE MUSEUM

1572 Columbia St., San Diego
(619) 232-FIRE

Kids are as fond of firetrucks as they are about peanut butter and jelly. So take your tykes to the Firehouse Museum located in San Diego's oldest firehouse. More than a half-dozen fire engines decorate the place, including an 1841 six-man, hand-pumped steamer, a 1903 three-horse-drawn steamer and a 1922 Stutz. The helmet collection from around the world is impressive. Don't miss the melted helmet mounted on the wall, it's a visual reminder to kids about the dangers of fire.

Children enjoy gazing up at the spiral stairs and the long pole firefighters once slid down. With models, uniforms, vintage photos, badge and alarm collections and other artifacts, the Museum educates and inspires appreciation for the profession that has come a long way in the past 100 years. For example, check out the oldest fire extinguisher on display; a leather bucket (directions for use: fill, pour on fire, repeat). School group tours by arrangement.

SEASONS AND TIMES
➤ Year-round: Sat and Sun, 10 am—4 pm.

COST

➤ Adults $2, seniors, military and youth (13 to 17) $1, under 13 free.

GETTING THERE

➤ By car, from Interstate 5 south, exit Sassafrass St. Turn east on Cedar, south on Columbia. Metered street parking. About 10 minutes from Old Town.

➤ By public transit, take the Blue Line trolley to County Administration Trolley Station and walk east to Columbia St.

COMMENT

➤ Plan a 1-hour visit.

Ships Ahoy!
MARITIME MUSEUM

1306 North Harbor Dr., San Diego
(619) 234-9153
www.sdmaritime.com

Clamber aboard not one, but three historic vessels anchored along the Embarcadero on the edge of downtown San Diego to experience the Maritime Museum. The *Berkeley*, a ferryboat that served on San Francisco Bay from 1898 to 1958, is now home to the admission desk, gift shop and exhibits depicting maritime history with models, maps, narratives, photographs and artifacts. Kids enjoy going below to the engine and boiler rooms—just beware of the steep steps. Adjacent to the *Berkeley* is the *Medea*, a 1904 steam yacht with elegant oak woodwork and period furnishings viewable in the saloon, bed and dining areas.

Steps away is the *Star of India*, an 1863 full-rigged and iron-hulled ship. Be sure to explore all decks. Up top, appreciate the view of San Diego Bay and the ship's baffling number of sails and ropes. Down below see the cargo hold and changing special exhibits including Pirates—featuring everything from the skull of Blackbeard to the lovable characters of *Muppet Treasure Island*. On the middle deck, see the cramped quarters of Swedish emigrants who crossed to New Zealand aboard the *Star of India* in the 1870s. Explain to your kids that this ship has survived mutiny and collisions, heavy storms and at least 21 trips around the world. And since she still takes to the high seas every few years, she's considered the oldest ship still sailing in the world.

The Museum's setting alone is worthy, with the sea lapping along the docks on one side and San Diego's skyline on the other. Cruise ships and Navy vessels are frequently docked and in easy sight. You'll find plenty of food and souvenirs in the surrounding Embarcadero area. Walk or take a pedicab about 1.8-miles farther south along Harbor Drive and visit quaint Seaport Village (page 59).

SEASONS AND TIMES
➤ Year-round: Daily, 9 am—8 pm.

COST
➤ Adults $6, seniors (over 62), military and youth (13 to 17) $4, children (6 to 12) $2, under 6 free.

GETTING THERE
➤ By car, from Interstate 5 south, exit Ash St. Follow west to Harbor Dr., turn south. Metered parking along Harbor Dr. About 15 minutes from Old Town.

➤ By public transit, ride the Blue Line trolley to Santa Fe Depot and walk two blocks west.
➤ By bike or on foot, head south along the water from Seaport Village or take Broadway heading west and follow car directions. Bike racks available.

NEARBY
➤ Chinese Historical Museum, Coronado, Firehouse Museum, Gaslamp Quarter, Seaport Village.

COMMENT
➤ Plan a 2-hour visit. Some areas of the *Berkeley* are wheelchair accessible. No strollers.

Hear the Bells?
MISSION SAN DIEGO DE ALCALA

10818 San Diego Mission Rd., San Diego
(619) 281-8449

Y ou can hear the bells ring out everyday from the Companario, the often-pictured white adobe tower that houses five bells at Mission de Alcala. Founded by Father Junipero Serra, this was the first of 21 missions established in California. Today this National Historical Landmark encompasses a museum, gardens, archaeological ruins and California's first church—originally built in 1769.

Step inside the church and view the hand-painted 29-foot high wood beam ceilings, meticulously restored to the beauty of its earliest days. The enchanting garden includes bougainvillea, aloe vera, roses and saintly statues. Kids will want to toss a coin in the St. Francis Wishing Well, or try their hand at using the matates (grinding tools used by early Natives) located in the courtyard. Thousands of artifacts representing various eras at the Mission were excavated from the ruins, many of which now reside in the Museum. Native American, farming and religious artifacts are on display, as well as spurs, stirrups, military swords and saddle flasks circa the 1800s. There are no picnic areas and bringing food onto the Mission grounds is discouraged. Call ahead for handicapped parking/access instructions. Tote-a-Tape tours available for $2. Group tours by arrangement.

SEASONS AND TIMES
➤ Year-round: Daily, 9 am—4:45 pm. Closed Christmas and New Year's.

COST
➤ Adults $3, seniors and students $2, under 12 free.

GETTING THERE
➤ By car, from Hwy. 163 or Interstate 5, take Interstate 8 east to Mission Gorge Rd. Turn north and follow to Twain Ave. Turn west on Twain, which becomes San Diego Mission Rd. Free parking. About 10 minutes from Old Town.
➤ By public transit, ride the Blue Line trolley to Mission San Diego.

COMMENT
➤ Plan a 1-hour visit. Diaper-changing facilities available. Some areas are difficult for wheelchairs and strollers.

Old Fashioned Fun at
OLD POWAY PARK

14134 Midland Rd., Poway
(858) 679-4313
www.ci.poway.ca.us/oldpoway
www.powaymidlandrr.org

This living historic village transports kids back to a time when the West was still wild. From the 1894 yellow trolley to the 1907 Baldwin steam locomotive, from the blacksmith's shop to the Heritage Museum, a trip to Old Poway Park is sure to be jam-packed with smiles—and an appreciation of the past.

Amidst the restored historic buildings and picnic areas in this five-acre park, the Poway-Midland Railroad runs its trains every weekend. For an extra-special treat, be sure to visit at Christmas when Santa arrives by locomotive! If examining artifacts is more your thing, stop at Nelson House that was built in 1909 and is furnished with period pieces, or visit the blacksmith's shop on Saturdays. At the Heritage Museum, see displays of Native American artifacts and an array of antique farm tools, historical photographs reflecting local history and exhibits that depict the old school house, post office and general store. Point out the scrub board and butter churn—your kids will gain an appreciation for the ease of 21st century chores.

Templars Hall, circa 1896, sits next to grassy lawns studded with oak trees (great for climbing) and equipped with tables and barbecues for a family picnic. Or avoid the hassle and eat at the Hamburger Factory restaurant. The funky western theme is fun for families while eating breakfast, lunch or dinner. Holidays at the park are taken seriously, so be sure to call ahead for a fun-filled schedule of events. Organized group tours for schools, Scout troops and seniors available.

SEASONS AND TIMES
➤ Park: Year-round, daily, dawn—dusk. Train rides: Year-round, Sat, 10 am—4 pm; Sun, 11 am—2 pm. Closed second Sunday of each month. Museum: Year-round, Sat and Sun, 9 am—4 pm.

COST
➤ Park: Free. Train rides: Adults $2, children (under 12) 50 cents. Museum: Free. Donations accepted.

GETTING THERE
➤ By car from Interstate 15, exit at Poway Rd. and head east. At Midland Rd., turn north. Follow to Park, located on the west side. Free parking. About 35 minutes from Old Town.

NEARBY
➤ Poway Lake Park.

COMMENT
➤ Plan a 3-hour visit.

Battle Cry
SAN PASQUAL
BATTLEFIELD STATE PARK

15808 San Pasqual Valley Rd., Escondido
(760) 489-0076
www.parks.ca.gov

The Mexican-American War—when the words lie flat in a history book, they're pretty ho-hum. But take children to the actual site of one of the fiercest battles of 1846, and history suddenly doesn't seem so distant. Exhibits within the Visitor Center explain the Native American, Spanish, Mexican and American occupations of the area and include a realistic diorama. A map of the battle is featured in the observation room, helping to relay how the battle progressed day by day. The short video is worthwhile, outlining the Mexican-American War.

Outside you'll overlook the now peaceful grounds—the actual battle site where 160 U.S. soldiers attacked Mexican forces at the Village of San Pasqual. Nearby the recreated American Soldier's campsite is an especially intriguing addition for children. Hike the half-mile self-guided nature trail, located just behind the center. If you're up for a little more, continue your trek west across Battle Monument Trail, where you will find a ramada and bench for lovely views of the valley (about one mile round trip). Within the 50-acre park, there are also picnic tables and an amphitheater. Reenactments of the battle take place annually, call the Visitor Center for more information or for group tour information.

SEASONS AND TIMES
➤ Year-round: Daily, dawn—dusk. Visitor Center: Fri—Sun, 10 am—5 pm.

COST
➤ Free.

GETTING THERE
➤ By car, take Interstate 15 north to Via Rancho Parkway Exit. Travel east to San Pasqual Rd., then turn east again at State Hwy. 78. Located about one mile past the Wild Animal Park. Free parking. About 40 minutes from Old Town.

NEARBY
➤ California Center for the Arts, Wild Animal Park.

COMMENT
➤ Plan a 2-hour visit. Diaper-changing facilities available.

Victorian Grandeur
VILLA MONTEZUMA

1925 K St., San Diego
(619) 239-2211
www.sandiegohistory.org

While the surrounding neighborhood is somewhat shabby, Villa Montezuma rises up from the sidewalk like a surreal, sensational dream. Smokestacks, spindled trim, stained glass windows and griffins decorate the turrets and towers, awing visitors before they step through the doors.

Villa Montezuma, also known as the Jesse Shepard House, was built of Victorian excess in 1887. Shepard was an acclaimed pianist who held concerts in the house and hung out with the rich and famous, and Russian royalty of his day. The house is considered one of the finest examples of Victorian architecture on the West Coast. Its walls are polished redwood with a staggering number of art glass windows. The house has five fireplaces and luxurious furnishings reflecting Turkish, Asian, European and other worldly influences. The portrait windows were custom-made for Shepard by special technique in San Francisco. They depict Beethoven, Mozart, Rubens, Raphael and others. Detailed woodwork, tile work and other embellishments make every room a masterpiece.

Kids delight in the dumb waiter and voice tube (where Shepard ordered and received his dinner), and appreciate the kitchen full of Victorian-era gadgets. You can touch the pieces and attempt to guess their use. Tours (held daily) are about 45 minutes and will keep kids interested. Old Town Trolley Tours (page 160) hosts a seasonal Ghosts and Gravestones tour that stops at the Villa Montezuma to share a few ghostly tales. Also every year, the Villa holds a Victorian tea in February and dons its Christmas finery beginning December 1. Call ahead for group arrangements.

SEASONS AND TIMES
➤ Year-round: Fri—Sun, 10 am—4:30 pm.

COST
➤ Adults $5, seniors, students and active military $4, children (6 to 17) $2, under 6 free.

GETTING THERE
➤ By car, from Interstate 5 south, exit at Imperial Ave., turning east. Turn north on Nineteenth Ave. and east on K St. Street parking. About 10 minutes from Old Town.
➤ By public transit, take bus route 5A to stop at Market St. and Nineteenth St. Walk south to K St.

NEARBY
➤ Coronado, Gaslamp Quarter.

COMMENT
➤ Plan a 1-hour visit. No wheelchairs or strollers allowed.

OTHER HISTORICAL SITES

BANCROFT RANCH HOUSE MUSEUM
9050 Memory Lane, Spring Valley
(619) 469-1480
An 1863 adobe ranch home that houses period furnishings, photographs and archives. Lawn area with picnic tables, pepper trees and friendly chickens. Free.

GRAPE DAY PARK-HERITAGE WALK
321 North Broadway, Escondido
(760) 743-8207
A collection of buildings dating back as far as 1888, including examples of a Victorian home, railroad station and library. Donations accepted.

HERITAGE PARK
Heritage Park Row, San Diego
(619) 291-3393
A smattering of Victorian buildings above Old Town. Site of superb annual Egg Hunt. Free.

MISSION SAN LUIS REY DE FRANCIA

4050 Mission Rd., Oceanside

(760) 757-3651

Lovely historic grounds and museum chronicling Spanish
colonization and life at the Mission. Adults $3, children (6 to 15)
$1, under 6 free.

MOUNT WOODSON CASTLE

16422 N. Woodson Ave., Ramona

(760) 789-7644

A 12,000-square-foot, 27-room architectural wonder built in 1921
for an eccentric dress designer named Amy Strong. The home's
design is an odd, but exquisite blend of English cottage, French
castle and windmills from the Netherlands.

STEIN FARM

1808 F Ave., National City

(619) 426-5109

The 1890 house is restored with period pieces. Antique farm
equipment, livestock tack, trucks, wagons and more in original
condition. Carekeeper tours take you to meet resident farm animals and to sample produce from the orchard. Weekends only and
school groups by arrangement. Picnic area. Donations accepted.

CHAPTER 9

GETTING THERE IS HALF THE FUN

Introduction

There are so many exciting ways for families to get around San Diego. From biking to bus tours to hot air ballooning, it's no surprise the journey often is a joyous part of the destination. For little eyes and ears, the seemingly mundane—boarding the bus, for example—becomes an adventure in itself. Don't be surprised if the sites listed in this chapter turn out to be some of your tykes' favorite activities. After all, who doesn't love the clanging of a trolley, the liberating feel of pedaling a bicycle, riding in a carriage pulled by horses, sailing the open sea or soaring through the sky in a balloon?

Be sure to spend lots of time exploring San Diego's varied, clever and very unique modes of transportation—because getting there really is half the fun.

Ride the Rails
AMTRAK TRAINS

Santa Fe Depot
1050 Kettner Blvd., San Diego
(800) 872-7245
www.amtrak.com

Eager engineers in your family will love this trip—riding the rails on San Diego's Amtrak. Depart from the Santa Fe Depot (a 1915 Spanish Colonial station) aboard a double-decker diesel locomotive painted bright blue and green for a short commuter trip (800-COASTER) to Del Mar or Carlsbad (about $3 one way). Or, pint-sized passengers can chug all the way to Los Angeles and destinations beyond aboard Amtrak trains, offering such kid-friendly amenities as free activity books, junior engineer caps, movie and cartoon videos and complimentary cookies and milk. Kids always ride for half-price with Amtrak, but call or visit the website for details and other specials. Visit the exhibits and small gift shop inside the Depot operated by the San Diego Railroad Museum for an educational enhancement to your venture.

SEASONS AND TIMES
➤ Year-round: Daily.

COST
➤ Adults $44 (round-trip to Los Angeles). Discounts for children. Call or visit the website for details and other destination fares.

GETTING THERE

➤ By car, travel Interstate 5 south to Front St. Go south on Broadway. Located on north side of street, before Pacific Hwy. Free parking. About 10 minutes from Old Town.

➤ By public transit, take the Blue Line trolley to the Santa Fe Depot.

NEARBY

➤ Gaslamp Quarter, Maritime Museum, Firehouse Museum, Seaport Village, Coronado, Villa Montezuma, Balboa Park, San Diego Zoo.

COMMENT

➤ Plan an 2-hour trip to Los Angeles.

Look Mom, No Hands!
BICYCLE &
PEDICAB TOURS

A great way to get around parts of San Diego—particularly the beach areas and downtown—is by bicycle. You can rent bicycles ranging from mountain bikes to beach cruisers and tandem rides. Better yet, relax and let someone else do the pedaling. Pedicab tours are a great way to take in the town and conveniently shuttle between Seaport Village, the Embarcadero and Gaslamp Quarter (page 19).

Family biking is best along Mission Bay (page 122), Coronado Tidelands Park trail, or on the scenic route from Seaport Village heading north along Harbor Drive. Consult the experts below for other family-friendly bike routes.

BIKES AND BEYOND

1201 First St., Coronado
(619) 435-7180
www.hollandsbicycles.com
Bikes of all types and sizes for rent, as well as surrey and skate
rentals.

BIKE TOURS SAN DIEGO

509 Fifth Ave., San Diego
(619) 238-2444
www.bike-rentals.com
Provides bike rentals, bike maps and organized tours.

CALIFORNIA BICYCLE INC.

7462 La Jolla Blvd., La Jolla
(858) 454-0316
www.calbike.com

GASLAMP BICYCLE AND PEDICAB COMPANY

523 Island Ave., San Diego
(619) 595-0211
Bike tours, rentals and pedicab service for surrounding area.

MISSION BEACH CLUB

Ocean Front Walk, near the roller coaster in Mission Beach.
(858) 488-5050
Rent bikes, blades, scooters, boogie and surfboards by the hour,
day or week. Located on the boardwalk in action-packed Mission
Beach just north of Belmont Park.

THE ORIGINAL BIKE CAB COMPANY

(888) BIKECAB
www.bikecab.com
Professional bike tours, rentals and pedicab tours to popular
destinations.

On the Water
BOAT TOURS AND OTHER AQUATIC ADVENTURES

San Diego is surrounded by surf, so what would you expect? There are dozens of ways to get on the water. Take a brunch cruise with Hornblower, gather up the clan for a deep-sea fishing adventure, or take a tranquil gondola cruise. For a slow and steady trip, hop aboard the ferry between Seaport Village and Coronado. This one-hour round trip is the perfect introduction for hesitant sailors. Whatever watery adventure you choose, pack sweaters for the kids and call ahead to find out if you need to make reservations. And don't worry; life vests are always provided.

HORNBLOWER CRUISES
1066 N. Harbor Dr., San Diego
(619) 686-8700 or (800) ONTHEBAY
www.hornblower.com
One or two-hour harbor tours that highlight Navy vessels, the *Star of India*, Coronado Bridge, Shelter Island and Hotel del Coronado. Also offers private charters, nightly dinner dance cruises, seasonal whale watching and Sunday brunch.

H & M LANDING
2803 Emerson St., San Diego
(619) 222-1144
www.hmlanding.com
The place to go for sport fishing adventure is the open sea. Part-, full- and multi-day trips. Seasonal whale watching and private charters available.

LA JOLLA KAYAK & CO.

2199 Avenida de la Playa, La Jolla
(858) 459-1114
www.lajollakayak.com
Paddle through the incredible caves of La Jolla. Picnic packages, snorkeling, groups, all ages welcome.

MISSION BAY SPORTCENTER

1010 Santa Clara Place, San Diego
(858) 488-1004
www.missionbaysportcenter.com
An exceptional site to learn a new sport that provides rental and instruction in sailing, wind surfing, kayaking, water-skiing, surfing and more.

SAN DIEGO CORONADO FERRY

1050 N. Harbor Dr., San Diego
(619) 234-4111 or (800) 442-7847
www.harborexcursion.com
Provides hourly ferry service between the Broadway Pier near Seaport Village and charming Ferry Landing Marketplace on Coronado.

SAN DIEGO HARBOR EXCURSION

1050 N. Harbor Dr., San Diego
(619) 234-4111 or (800) 442-7847
www.harborexcursion.com
Informative narrated one- or two-hour harbor tours, as well as dinner cruises, whale watching and more. Indoor seating as well as spacious sun decks.

SEAFORTH LANDING

1641 Quivira Rd., San Diego
www.seaforthboatrental.com
Rents sailboats, jet skis, speedboats and more (instruction available), plus fishing charters, sunset sails, and seasonal whale watching.

THE GONDOLA COMPANY

4000 Coronado Bay Rd., Coronado
(619) 429-6317
www.gondolacompany.com
A trip through the waterways of Coronado via gondola.

Wheels on the Bus
BUS AND
TROLLEY TOURS

B us tours are often the best way to introduce your family to a city you've never experienced. There are several options to choose from, but all have knowledgeable guides and allow you to relax instead of driving through an unfamiliar city. The Zoo, SeaWorld and Coronado are most often included on the tour, but some companies will escort you north into Los Angeles or as far south as Tijuana, Mexico. Many offer hop on, hop off service and multi-day tickets. Kids especially enjoy double decker buses.

For a very special tour providing flexible family fun, ride the Old Town Trolley buses (designed to look like trolley cars). Talented "historytellers" relate San Diego's past and toss in little-known facts and funny anecdotes. The green and orange trolleys make a continuous loop, stopping at each popular destination every 30 minutes. Old Town Trolley Tours also offers a "frightseeing" tour for a night time trip to some of San Diego's spookier haunts and an exclusive Navy Base Tour.

To plan a trip on a MTS (Metropolitan Transit System) bus, use their convenient website with interactive trip planner at www.sdcommute.com or call (800) 266-6883.

COACH USA/GRAYLINE SAN DIEGO
1775 HANCOCK ST., SAN DIEGO
(619) 491-0011

www.graylinesandiego.com

Offers a San Diego city tour and trips to the Zoo, SeaWorld, Seaport Village and Harbor Cruise. Mexico adventures available as well.

CONTACTOURS & CHARTER SERVICES
1726 Wilson Ave., National City

(619) 477-8687

www.contactours.com

Daily narrated tours to Legoland, San Diego Zoo, the Wild Animal Park and more. Complimentary hotel pick-up and return.

DOUBLE DECKER BUS & TOURS
1410/A Broadway, Chula Vista

(619) 702-9100

www.double-decker-buses.com

San Diego tours, shuttle service and special occasion charters aboard 70-passenger double-decker buses.

OLD TOWN TROLLEY TOURS
(619) 298-8687

www.historictours.com

SAN DIEGO SCENIC TOURS
3-2255 Garnet Ave., San Diego

(858) 273-8687

Small, personal daily tours of San Diego, La Jolla, Coronado and Tijuana.

Clippity Clop
CINDERELLA CARRIAGE COMPANY

801 W. Market St., San Diego
(619) 239-8080
www.cinderella-carriage.com

Perhaps even better than seeing a beautiful steed pulling an elegant white carriage through the streets is hearing the clippity clop of hooves echoing on the pavement.

The Cinderella Carriage Company serves up this old-fashioned form of transportation, offering rides through San Diego's downtown, along the Bay or through the historic Gaslamp Quarter (page 19). Kids especially thrill to the experience, and rides begin at only $25. The Company happily makes arrangements for children's birthday parties, weddings and other special events.

Catch a carriage ride from the front of the Harbor House restaurant in Seaport Village or at the Gaslamp Quarter Depot at Fifth and F Streets downtown. The adjacent Carriage Stop Café sells pastries, coffees and specialty drinks with such names as Prince Charming and Fairy Godmother. Carriage ride reservations available.

SEASONS AND TIMES
➤ Seaport Village Stand: Daily, 11 am–midnight. Gaslamp Quarter Depot: Daily, 6 pm–midnight.

COST
➤ $25 to $80 per ride (not per person), dependent on length of route.

GETTING THERE
➤ By car to Seaport Village Stand, follow Interstate 5 south to Front St. Exit. Go west on Ash St., then south on Pacific Hwy. and follow to Seaport Village. By car to Gaslamp Quarter Depot, take Interstate 5 south to Front St., go east on Broadway, then south on 4th Ave. Proceed to F St. Area parking. About 10 minutes from Old Town (either stop).

NEARBY
➤ Gaslamp Quarter, Coronado, San Diego Zoo, Firehouse Museum, Maritime Museum, Chinese Historical Museum, Villa Montezuma.

COMMENT
➤ Rides range from 15 minutes to 1 hour.

Little Red
SAN DIEGO TROLLEY

(800) COMMUTE or (619) 231-8549
www.sdcommute.com

These bright red trolleys roll merrily through Mission Valley, the Gaslamp, East County and the South Bay. The electric trolleys run along two routes (referred to as the Blue Line and the Orange Line), transporting people through the city to many popular destinations.

In addition to being uncrowded, inexpensive

and non-polluting, the trolleys are a great source of entertainment for kids. The Blue Line scoots between Qualcomm Stadium, Mission Valley (with easy access to Mission de Alcala, malls and restaurants), Old Town and the International Mexico Border. The Orange Line runs out to cities east of San Diego, such as El Cajon and Santee, as well as stopping at stations situated at Seaport Village, the Gaslamp Quarter and the Convention Center. Visit the Transit Store (102 Broadway, 619-234-1060) downtown for tickets and information. Tickets can also be purchased at station vending machines (some require exact change).

SEASONS AND TIMES
➤ Year-round: Daily, 5 am—6 pm (15 minute schedules); nightly, 6 pm—1 am (30 minute schedules).

COST
➤ Adults $1 to $2.25, senior citizens and disabled 75 cents, children under 6 free. Price depends on distance traveled.

GETTING THERE
➤ There are over 40 stations where you can hop aboard the trolley. Call the above phone number or visit the website for more information.

COMMENT
➤ Blue Line trolley stop located in Old Town Transit Center.

Soaring Above San Diego
SKY RIDES

For high-flying fanatics, soaring through the skies is a fabulous way to spend an afternoon. Whether it's in a colorful hot air balloon or aboard a World War II air bird, enjoy breathtaking aerial views of San Diego's beautiful landscapes and coastline by making reservations at any one of the places listed below.

A BALLOON ADVENTURE
F, 162 S. Rancho Santa Fe Rd., Encinitas
(760) 438-3344
www.californiadreamin.com
Float above beautiful San Diego in a hot air balloon. Sunrise and sunset flights daily.

BALLOON FLIGHTS, LLC
15255 El Camino Real, Rancho Santa Fe
(858) 756-6967
www.sunballoon.com
Sunset balloon flights over Del Mar. Picnic packages available.

BARNSTORMING ADVENTURES
Mc-Clellan Palomar Airport
2198 Palomar Airport Rd., Carlsbad
(800) 759-5667
www.barnstorming.com
Unique flying adventures offered aboard vintage planes. Try the thrilling "Top Dog Air Combat" packages simulating aerial battle. One-hundred percent safety record, FAA approved. Reservations required.

CORPORATE HELICOPTERS
3753 John Montgomery Dr., San Diego
(858) 505-5650
www.corporatehelicopters.com
Provides scenic helicopter tours and charter flights.

CHAPTER 10

FAVORITE
FESTIVALS

Introduction

Want an excuse to celebrate? In San Diego, nearly every week or weekend in every month of the year, you can find a special celebration. Most are family-oriented and many are free. From country fun during Lakeside Western Days to the polka pride of Oktoberfest, there's a variety of things to do and cultures to learn about. While the San Diego County Fair welcomes hundreds of thousands of visitors annually, the relatively small Ocean Beach Kite Festival provides a relaxed day of kite-flying along the shore. Check the Directory of Events for more annual happenings—and keep celebrating!

The Hills Are Alive!
CARLSBAD
FLOWER FIELDS

5704 Paseo del Norte, Carlsbad
(760) 431-0352
www.theflowerfields.com

It only lasts about seven weeks a year, so hustle to the flower fields to get an annual treat unlike any other. Fifty acres of brilliant ranunculus flowers burst into full bloom to comprise these famous fragrant fields. They have fascinated the public for sixty years, so growers have developed tours and educational programs.

School and senior groups can enjoy guided tours and hay wagon rides, including special instruction regarding the history of the fields, the growing process, and flower varieties. Other educational programs include classroom presentations, as well as an art program and a composting program. Also, there are student activity sheets to download from the website. Visit the garden center and gift shop at the fields and take a little of the beauty home with you. Guided walking tours are about 45 minutes and cost $8 (instead of the regular $5 admission charge). Call ahead for group arrangements.

SEASONS AND TIMES
➤ Spring (early Mar—early May): Daily, 9 am—5 pm.

COST
➤ Adults $5, seniors (60 and over) $4, children (3 to 10) $3, under 3 free.

GETTING THERE
➤ By car, take Interstate 5 north to Palomar Airport Road Exit. Turn east and drive one block to Paseo Del Norte and turn north. Parking lot on east side. About 45 minutes from Old Town.

NEARBY
➤ Legoland, Museum of Making Music.

COMMENT
➤ Plan a 1 ½-hour visit. Wear comfortable closed-toe walking shoes.

...But Once a Year
CHRISTMAS
ON THE PRADO

Balboa Park, San Diego
(619) 239-0512 or (619) 231-1640
www.balboapark.org

Held in beautiful Balboa Park, this seasonal celebration occurs the first weekend in December. For two evenings each year, the park sparkles with festive music, dancing, food and performances. All of the Museums within the park open their doors free of charge and stage some type of fun, be it Victorian carolers, a bell choir, or bratwurst and beer gardens.

Around the park, you'll find chestnuts roasting on an open fire, folk dancers, a Santa Lucia procession and varied musical acts—from Brazilian flute troupes to blues bands. Sensational foods simmer at the International Cottages, where everyone lines up to purchase tasty treats from around the globe. Shop for unique gifts at the varied museum gift shops and specialty booths.

Friendly animals from the zoo visit the Kids Zone (located on the south end of the park near the Automotive Museum), where there are kids activities and performances. Parking is tight, so the earlier you arrive the better. Free shuttles transport from Zoo and City College lots on Park Blvd.

SEASONS AND TIMES
➤ First weekend in Dec: Fri—Sat, 5 pm—9 pm.

COST
➤ Free. Food and gifts for sale.

GETTING THERE
➤ By car, from Hwy. 163 south, exit at Park Blvd. and head north. Some parking available in the park and surrounding area, otherwise use lots with free shuttle service at the Zoo or at City College (south on Park Blvd.). About 10 minutes from Old Town.
➤ By public transit, take bus route 7/7A/7B to stop at Park Blvd. and Village Place. Walk southwest into Balboa Park.

NEARBY
➤ Chinese Historical Museum, Gaslamp Quarter, San Diego Zoo, Seaport Village, Coronado, Villa Montezuma.

COMMENT
➤ Plan a 2-hour visit. Arrive early. Crowds make wheelchair/stroller access difficult.

Old Glory
FLEET WEEK

San Diego Chamber of Commerce, San Diego
(619) 544-1387
www.sdfleetweek.org

Wear your red, white and blue proudly for seven days in October. Fleet Week serves up star-spangled events throughout San Diego—a town with a strong military history and even stronger patriotism.

One of the most popular events is the three-day Miramar Air Show, the largest Military Air Show in America. Thousands of families gather to watch the Blue Angels perform amazing feats overhead at the Marine Corps Air Station at Miramar. Also on-site are food booths, entertainment and opportunities to tour and touch aircraft.

At the Chrysler Jeep Speed Festival, held one weekend in Coronado, vintage car races thrill spectators. Colossal Navy ships at Broadway Pier also welcome the public aboard for tours throughout much of the Fleet Week celebration. Parades and fireworks dot the schedule of these very-American activities. Costs and locations vary, so call or visit the website for complete information and a schedule of events.

SEASON AND TIMES
➤ Mid-Oct.

COST
→ Some events are free.

Yee-Haw!
LAKESIDE WESTERN DAYS AND RODEO

Hwy. 67 and Mapleview, Lakeside
(619) 561-1031
www.lakesideca.com

Pull on 'yer boots and mosey on over to the greatest collection of Western fun under the San Diego sun. Three solid days of whooping it up happens every spring, including a roaring rodeo featuring calf roping, bull riding and barrel racing. Beyond the rodeo, the surrounding little town of Lakeside bursts at the seams with a Western Days festival filled with country-western bands, children's activities, and food and craft booths.

There's lots of western wear for sale in case your chaps have worn thin or you've misplaced your ten-gallon hat. On Saturday, there's a parade along nearby Woodside and Maine Ave. Kids will enjoy the clowns, but the event is especially pleasing to horse lovers and aspiring cowpokes. For specific rodeo information, visit www.lakesiderodeo.com.

SEASONS AND TIMES

➤ Late Apr: Fri–Sun, 9 am–5 pm. Call for exact dates and current schedule of events.

COST

➤ Western Days Festival: Free. Rodeo: Adults $8 to $11, under 12 free.

GETTING THERE

➤ By car, travel Interstate 8 east to Hwy. 67 north. Follow to freeway's end at Mapleview. Turn east and watch for signs. Parking on site. About 35 minutes from Old Town.

COMMENT

➤ Plan to spend 2 hours. Only portable restrooms available outside the rodeo.

High Flying Fun
OCEAN BEACH KITE FESTIVAL

4726 Santa Monica Ave., San Diego
(619) 531-1527

At this salute to spring festival, activities begin at the Ocean Beach Recreation Center where kids craft their own kites. All materials are provided and there's plenty of help available. Blue ribbons are awarded for the Most Original, Best Decorated and other categories. Participants receive a free hot dog, punch and popcorn and are invited to march down Newport

Avenue (Ocean Beach's equivalent to Main St.) for a kid's parade to the nearby beach. Then the mosaic of colorful kites take to the skies for an afternoon of high-flying fun. A craft fair also offers lots of homespun shopping near the recreational center. Ensure kids arrive in the morning to allow time for kite building.

SEASONS AND TIMES
➤ First Sat in Mar: 9 am—3 pm. Call for exact schedule.

COST
➤ Free.

GETTING THERE
➤ By car, take Interstate 8 heading west and follow to Sunset Cliffs Blvd. Proceed south to Santa Monica Blvd., turn east. Street parking. About 10 minutes from Old Town.
➤ By public transit, take bus route 35A to stop at Cable St. and Santa Monica Ave. Walk southeast to the recreation center.

NEARBY
➤ SeaWorld.

COMMENT
➤ Plan to spend the day.

Oom-Pah-Pah and Pretzels
OKTOBERFEST

La Mesa Blvd., La Mesa
(619) 465-7700
www.eastcountychamber.org

A German festival patterned after the world-famous celebration in Munich, Oktoberfest closes down several streets of the quaint downtown "village" of La Mesa, to put on a much-anticipated annual party. Literally hundreds of booths fill the streets, offering varied items for sale and tummy-tempting foods (kids favor the warm pretzels while parents like to sample the sauerkraut). The entertainment is fun and the community spirited—with om-pah-pah bands, traditional German costumes and folk dancing performances. The dance floors are open and inviting to "kids" of all ages, and there are many group participation dances and activities. Taking the trolley is encouraged due to limited parking.

SEASONS AND TIMES
➤ Generally the first weekend in October. Call for exact dates and times.

COST
➤ Free.

GETTING THERE
➤ By car, take Interstate 8 east to Spring St. Drive south to La Mesa Blvd. or Allison St. and look for area parking. About 15 minutes from Old Town.

➤ By public transit, ride the Orange Line trolley and exit at La Mesa Blvd. station.

COMMENT

➤ Plan a 2-hour visit. Portable restrooms only.

Ferris Wheels to Funnel Cakes
SAN DIEGO COUNTY FAIR

**2260 Jimmy Durante Blvd., Del Mar
(858) 755-1161 or (858) 793-5555
www.delmarfair.com**

The San Diego County Fair (formerly known as the Del Mar Fair) welcomes over a million visitors each year between mid-June and July 4th. People of all ages flock to this fabulous festival for music, food, rides and more.

Interested in entertainment? Check out the big name acts at the Grandstand Stage (free with fair admission). Other shows go on throughout the day at the smaller stages, showcasing everything from tap dancing to racing swine. For more fun, watch live-stock competitions and auctions. Kids will beg to see the barns filled with sheep, cattle, horses, goats, chickens and pigs.

Exhibit halls display art, photography, gems and minerals, quilts, crafts, woodworking and more. Want to do something active? Enter a contest—there's the best animal noise contest, pie-eating contest and bubble gum blowing contest, among others. For teens, the Fun Zone has fanatical sky-high and raucous rides lifting you up for spine-tingling views of the Pacific. Kiddieland is the best for families, located in the racetrack infield and loaded with games, rides and exhibits, well suited for those 12 and under.

Food is of course, first-place fair fare, from corn dogs to cotton candy to fried zucchini. Ride tickets can be expensive, take advantage of any available bargains—Alberston's grocery stores sell Family Packs (includes admission, drink coupons and ride tickets at a low price) before the fair opens. Or show up on Kids Day (every Tuesday), where children under 13 are admitted free. Be sure to schedule a visit on July 4th to watch the festival end with phenomenal fireworks.

SEASONS AND TIMES
➤ Mid June—July 4: Sun—Thu, 10 am—10 pm. Fri—Sat, 10 am—11 pm. Call for current schedule.

COST
➤ Adults $9.50, seniors (62 and older) $6, children (6 to 12) $4.50, under 6 free.

GETTING THERE
➤ By car, take Interstate 5 north to Via de la Valle Exit. Travel Via de la Valle west to Jimmy Durante Blvd. and go south. Watch for entrance signs and parking attendants. Parking: Car $6, RV $7, Preferred $10. About 20 minutes from Old Town.
➤ For public transit information, call (800) 266-6883 for current fairground routes.

NEARBY
➤ Free Flight Aviary, Torrey Pines State Reserve.

COMMENT
➤ Plan to spend the day. Diaper changing facilities and lockers available.

Sandy Creations
U.S. OPEN SANDCASTLE COMPETITION

Seacoast Dr., Imperial Beach
(619) 424-6663
www.cityofib.com

Every July, thousands of families admire the astounding temporary works of art perched upon the sand—you'll certainly see castles, but also sharks, dragons, and other intricately designed flights of fancy. The largest sandcastle building competition in the country takes place annually on the shores of Imperial Beach. Saturday's events normally include a community pancake breakfast and a festive parade along Seacoast Drive to kick off the fun, followed by a low-key Kids-N-Castles contest for children. Sunday means serious competition where teams of builders vie for over $20,000 in cash prizes. Plentiful booths offer food and crafts, and live entertainment and fireworks propel the competition to full festival status.

SEASONS AND TIMES
➤ Generally the last weekend in July. Most events begin at 10 am and end at dusk. Call for current schedule.

COST
➤ Free.

GETTING THERE

➤ By car, take Interstate 5 south to Palm Ave. in Imperial Beach. Travel Palm Ave. west to Seacoast Dr. Turn south and continue toward Imperial Beach Pier. Limited parking. About 20 minutes from Old Town.

➤ By public transit, take the Blue Line trolley to Palm Ave. Trolley Station. Board bus 933 and travel to stop at Imperial Beach Blvd. and Seacoast Dr. Walk north toward the pier.

NEARBY

➤ Tijuana Estuary.

COMMENT

➤ Plan to spend 3 hours. No diaper changing facilities.

Room & Board
KID-FRIENDLY RESTAURANTS

Dining out with kids is no longer a hassle. Quite the contrary, thanks to kid-friendly eateries such the ones compiled below. These establishments serve up good food in an atmosphere welcoming good times, which means selections pleasing to kids' palates, scaled-down proportions, and enough surrounding ambiance and activity to keep children content.

Amenities such as high chairs and booster seats are available at the following locales and you can almost always count on activity menus and crayons to keep tykes busy, too. Go ahead, dine out more often. In these restaurants, the entire family will have a great time.

Great Breakfast Joints

HARRY'S COFFEE SHOP
(Kids' menu; serves sensational waffles with fresh fruit toppings, excellent omelets and more in fast-paced diner atmosphere; outdoor patio)
7545 Girard Ave., La Jolla (858) 454-7381.

THE BROKEN YOLK
(Kids' menu; huge portions; acclaimed omelets)
1851 Garnet Ave., San Diego (858) 270-9655

THE WAFFLE SPOT
(Kids' menu; chocolate-chip and banana split waffles and french toast planks; activity placemats; cartoon characters mural)
King's Inn Hotel, 1333 Hotel Circle South, San Diego (619) 297-2231.

THE ORIGINAL PANCAKE HOUSE
(Kids' activity menu; dozens of pancake varieties; fresh-squeezed juice)
3906 Convoy St., San Diego (858) 565-1740
160 S. Rancho Santa Fe Rd., San Diego (760) 943-1939
14905 Pomerado Rd., Poway (858) 679-0186

Favorite Family Eateries

CORVETTE DINER
(Kid's selections; outrageous shakes and desserts; authentic soda fountain; playful rock n' roll décor; retro music; participation sing and dance; homestyle American feel-good fare)
3946 Fifth Ave., San Diego (619) 542-1476

EL TORITO
(Comfy Mexican restaurant with good kids' food and activity menus)
8910 Via La Jolla Dr., La Jolla (858) 453-4115
271 Bay Blvd. West, Chula Vista (619) 425-6013
5024 Baltimore Dr., La Mesa (619) 698-7400
445 Camino del Rio South, San Diego (619)296-6154
8223 Mira Mesa Blvd., San Diego (858) 566-5792
2693 Vista Way, Oceanside (760) 439-5407
16375 Bernardo Center Dr., San Diego (858) 485-1905

FRIDAY'S
(Kids' activity menu; clamorous family atmosphere with a vast and varied menu; balloons; outdoor patio; keepable cups)
403 Camino del Rio South, San Diego (619) 297-8443
11650 Carmel Mountain Rd., San Diego (858) 675-7047
2991 Jamacha Rd., El Cajon (619) 670-7400
8801 Villa La Jolla Dr., La Jolla (858) 455-0880

FUDDRUCKER'S
(Kids' menu; ultra-casual with generous servings; arcade games;
and a tempting dessert counter)
8285 Mira Mesa Blvd., San Diego (858) 643-3916
5500 Grossmont Center Dr., La Mesa (619) 589-6144

ISLANDS
(Kids' activity menu; tropical-themed restaurants; with lush
greenery, colorful painted toucans; surf videos; awesome burgers,
chicken sandwiches and salads; keepable cups)
2441 Fenton Pkwy., San Diego (619) 640-2727
7637 Balboa Ave., San Diego (858) 569-8866
3351 Nobel Dr., San Diego (858) 455-9945
12224 Carmel Mountain Rd., San Diego (858) 485-8075

Classy Dinner and Kid Food, too!

ANTHONY'S FISH GROTTO
(Kids' menu; large, sparkling pond complete with ducks and
swans; shipwrecked boat with game room; keepable cups. San
Diego and Chula Vista locations have ocean views.)
9530 Murray Dr., La Mesa (619) 463-0368.
1360 Harbor Dr., San Diego (619) 232-5103
215 W. Bay Blvd., Chula Vista (619) 425-4200

BUCA DI BEPPO
(Kids' menu; delicious Italian fare served family-style amid funky
décor and fun waitstaff)
705 Sixth Ave., San Diego (619) 233-PAPA, www.bucadibeppo.com

CASA DE BANDINI
(Kids' menu; festive Mexican restaurant; large patio; bubbling
fountains; mariachis.
Old Town, San Diego (619) 297-8211

CLAIM JUMPER
(Kids' menu—prices based on children's weight; fun 1880s frontier
theme; huge portions specializing in steaks and ribs; kids' activity
book; kids' specialty drinks in keeper cups)
5500 Grossmont Center Dr., La Mesa (619) 469-3927
12384 Carmel Mountain Rd., San Diego (858) 485-8370

OLD SPAGHETTI FACTORY
(Kids' activity menu; vintage trolley car inside; superb pasta served
at low prices; kids' play corner in the waiting area; keepable cups)
275 Fifth Ave., San Diego (619) 233-4323, www.osf.com

And for Dessert...

FARRELL'S
(An old-time ice cream parlor specializing in sundaes, floats, malts;
birthday parties; candy shop and lunch and dinner menu, too)
10606 Camino Ruiz, Mira Mesa Shopping Center West, Suite 10,
San Diego (858) 578-9895

GHIRARDELLI SODA FOUNTAIN
(Assortment of ice cream creations; confections; gifts)
643 Fifth Ave., San Diego (619) 234-2449

FAMILY-FRIENDLY HOTELS

Family-friendly hotels give that "little extra
something" to make sure your stay is comfortable, especially for your littlest travelers.
From offering cribs at no charge to in-room
microwave ovens to complimentary breakfast bars,
many San Diego hotels anticipate traveling families' needs and go the extra mile to make sure
everyone's stay is enjoyable.

Be sure to inquire about special SeaWorld or San
Diego Zoo packages—many hotels can get discounted
tickets. The following hotels are all centrally located,
mostly in Mission Valley and the surrounding area,
and never more than about ten minutes from Old
Town and many of the great sites in this book. Most

offer seasonal discounts, weekend rates and family specials. And what's a San Diego stay without a pool? All the sites listed below have at least one splashing-blue pool!

value

HOTEL CIRCLE INN & SUITES
(Game room; discount attraction tickets; children's wading pool; barbeque grills; picnic tables; kitchen suites)
2201 Hotel Circle South, San Diego (619) 881-6800
www.hotelcircleinn.com

COMFORT SUITES
(Free breakfast buffet; game room; kids' suites with bunk beds, activity table and TV)
631 Camino del Rio South, San Diego (619) 881-4000

HOLIDAY INN EXPRESS
(Kids stay free; Complimentary breakfast bar; heated outdoor pool; in-room microwaves and refrigerators; complimentary shuttle service to SeaWorld)
3950 Jupiter St., San Diego (619) 226- 8000

Moderate

DOUBLETREE HOTEL
(Kids stay free; basket of fresh-baked cookies upon check-in; pool toys for kids)
7450 Hazard Center Dr., San Diego (619) 297-5466

HOLIDAY INN BAYSIDE
(Kids stay free; complimentary cribs; 2–hour bike rentals; ping-pong, shuffleboard; billiards; 9-hole putting course; kids under 12 eat free at adjacent Red Hen Country Kitchen)
4875 N. Harbor Dr., San Diego (619) 224-3621

TOWN & COUNTRY RESORT
(Kids stay free; family packages including Zoo, SeaWorld or Legoland tickets; gardens, four pools)
500 Hotel Circle N., San Diego (619) 291-7131
www.towncountry.com

Expensive

BAHIA RESORT HOTEL
(Summer family activities programs; children's playground; bike
rentals; Bahia Belle paddlewheeler cruises on Mission Bay)
3999 Mission Blvd., San Diego (888) 224-4273

HILTON SAN DIEGO RESORT
(Babysitting available; game room; in-room refrigerator;
Nintendo™; bike, skate and boat rentals)
1775 E. Mission Bay Dr., San Diego (619) 276-4010

SHERATON SAN DIEGO HOTEL & MARINA
(Kids stay free; 3 tropical pools; children's wading pool; game
room; complimentary cribs; in-room Nintendo™; bike and boat
rentals)
1380 Harbor Island Dr., San Diego (619) 692-2285

WESTIN HORTON PLAZA
(Kids' Club pack offers gift and coupons upon check-in;
babysitting available).
910 Broadway Circle, San Diego (619) 239-2200

12 Months of Fun
DIRECTORY OF EVENTS

JANUARY

Early January
San Diego Boat Show
San Diego Convention Center
111 W. Harbor Dr.
(619) 491-2475
www.boatshows.com

Early January to early March
Whale Watching
Islandia Sportfishing
1551 W. Mission Bay Dr.,
San Diego
(619) 222-1164
www.islandiasport.com

Mid-January
Martin Luther King, JR.
Parade and Festival
County Administration Building
1600 Pacific Hwy,
San Diego
(619) 264-0542

Late January
San Diego Marathon and 5K
Fun Run/Walk
Plaza Camino Real, Carlsbad
(858) 792-2900
www.sdmarathon.com

FEBRUARY

Early February
International Auto Show
San Diego Convention Center
111 W. Harbor Dr.
(619) 491-2475

Early February
Chinese New Year
Food and Cultural Fair
3rd and J St.
(619) 234-4447

MARCH

Mid-March
Saint Patrick's Day Parade
Sixth Ave. & Juniper St.,
San Diego
(619) 299-7812

Late March
MS Walk
Embarcadero Park, San Diego
Carlsbad Flower Fields, Carlsbad
(619) 974-8640

APRIL

Mid-April
Earth Fair
Balboa Park, San Diego
(619) 239-0512

Late April
Art Walk
Kettner Blvd., San Diego
(619) 615-1090
www.artwalkinfo.com

Saturday before Easter Sunday
Heritage Park Easter Egg Hunt
Heritage Park Row, San Diego
(858) 565-3600

Saturday before Easter Sunday
Gaslamp Easter Bonnet Parade
and Hat Contest
Fifth and L St., San Diego
(619) 238-6026

Easter Sunday
La Jolla Easter Hat Parade
Hershel & Prospect, La Jolla
(858) 454-2600

Late April
Wings Over Gillespie
Gillespie Field, El Cajon
(888) 215-7000

MAY

To late May
Buds n' Blooms
Balboa Park, San Diego
(619) 239-0512

Early May
Cinco de Mayo
Old Town, San Diego
(619) 220-5422

Mid-May
Pacific Beach Block Party and
Street Fair
Garnet Ave., San Diego
(619) 641-8823

Mid-May
Ramona Round-up Rodeo
Fifth & Aqua, Ramona
(760) 789-1484

JUNE

Early June
Indian Fair
Museum of Man
(619) 239-2001

Early to mid-June
Mainly Mozart Festival
Varied locations.
(619) 239-0100
www.mainlymozart.org

Mid-June
Dr. Seuss Run/Walk for Literacy
Seaport Village
849 W. Harbor Dr., San Diego
(858) 792-2900

Mid-June
Wooden Boat Festival
2303 Shelter Island Dr.
(619) 222-0981

Late June
Scottish Highland Games
1400 Vale Terrace Dr.,
Chula Vista
(619) 645-8080

JULY

Early July
Coronado Independence Day
Celebration
Varied Coronado sites.
(619) 437-8788

Mid-July
Festival of the Bells
Mission de Alcala
10818 San Diego Mission Rd.,
San Diego
(619) 283-7319

Mid-July
Pacific Islander Festival
Various San Diego locations
(619) 699-8797

Late July
Grunion Festival
On beach just south of Crystal
Pier in Pacific Beach, San Diego
(858) 274-1326

Late July
Comic-Con International
San Diego Convention Center
111 W. Harbor Dr., San Diego
(619) 491-2475

AUGUST

Early August
National City Automobile
Heritage Days
E. Twelfth St. & D St.,
National City
(619) 477-9339

Early to mid-August
Ringling Brothers,
Barnum & Bailey Circus
San Diego Sports Arena
3500 Sports Arena Blvd.,
San Diego
(619) 224-4171

SEPTEMBER

Early September
Street Scene
Gaslamp Quarter, San Diego
(619) 220-8497

Mid-September
International Friendship
Festival
El Cajon Civic Center
200 E. Main St., El Cajon
(619) 441-1753

Mid-September
Thunder Boat Racing
Mission Bay
Off Ingraham St., San Diego
(858) 268-1250

Late September
Cabrillo Festival
Cabrillo National Monument
1800 Cabrillo Memorial Dr.,
San Diego
(619) 557-5450

Late September
Poway Days Parade and Rodeo
Poway Rd. at Pomerado Rd.,
Poway
(858) 748-0016

OCTOBER

To late October
Kids Free Month
San Diego Zoo
2920 Zoo Dr., San Diego
(619) 234-3153

To late October
Haunted Hotel
424 Market St., San Diego
(619) 231-0131

To late October
Trail of Terror
Sixth Ave. & Juniper St.,
San Diego
(619) 231-0261

To late October
Scream Zone
Del Mar Fairgrounds
2260 Jimmy Durante Blvd.,
Del Mar
(858) 755-1161

Early to mid-October
Julian Fall Apple Harvest
Events throughout Julian
(760) 765-1857

Mid-October
Light the Night Against Crime
5K Walk/Run
Pacific Hwy. and Broadway,
San Diego
(858) 792-2900

Mid-October
Harvest Festival
San Diego Concourse
202 C St., San Diego
(800) 321-1213
www.harvestfestival.com

Mid-October
Miramar Air Show
Marine Corps Air Station
Miramar
(858) 577-1000

Late October
Underwater Pumpkin Carving
Contest
8200 Camino Del Oro, La Jolla
(858) 565-6054

NOVEMBER

Mid-November
Mother Goose Parade
W. Main St., Chambers and
Second St., El Cajon
(619) 444-8712

November 11th
Veteran's Day Parade
Harbor Dr., San Diego
(619) 239-2300

Late November
to early January
Del Mar Fairgrounds
Holiday of Lights
2260 Jimmy Durante Blvd.,
Del Mar
(858) 793-5555

DECEMBER

Early December
Las Posadas
Old Town, San Diego
(619) 220-5422

Early to late December
Victorian High Tea
Hotel Del Coronado
1500 Orange Ave., San Diego
(619) 435-6611

Early December
to early January
Wild Animal Park
Festival of Lights
15500 San Pasqual Valley Rd.,
Escondido
(760) 747-8702

Mid-December
San Diego Bay Parade of Lights
San Diego Bay
(619) 807-5262
www.sdparadeoflights.org

December 31st
First Night
Embarcadero Park, San Diego
(619) 296- 8731

INDEX

Aero Drive-in 99
Airplanes 82, 165
Amtrak 155
Amusement Parks 16, 21, 25, 51, 53, 59, 62, 177
Archeology 72, 144
Arco U.S. Olympic Training Center 81
Art Tours 39
Arts and Crafts 38, 43, 55, 67, 112, 173

Balboa Park 15, 170
Balloon Adventure 165
Balloon Flights, LLC 165
Balloon Rides 165
Bancroft Ranch House Museum 151
Barnes & Noble 33
Barnes Tennis Center 62
Barnstorming Adventures 165
Bates Nut Farm 113
Batter's Box 62
Beaches 17, 52, 123, 174, 179
Bell Gardens 105
Belmont Park 51
Bicycle Tours 156
Bicycling 16, 17, 51, 59, 123, 125, 126, 132, 133, 156, 179
Bike Tours San Diego 157
Bikes and Beyond 157
Birch Aquarium 65
Birthday Parties 22, 26, 34, 37, 41, 43, 54, 55, 56, 58, 61, 62, 66, 68, 76, 109, 112, 162
Boardwalk, The 62
Boat Cruises 158
Bookstar 34
Bookstores, Children's 33
Borders Books and Music 34
Bored? Skate Park 45

Bowling 34
Bright Valley Farms 114
Brown Bear Factory 39
Brunswick Premier Lanes 35
Buffalo Breath Costume Company 37
Bus Tours 160
Buses 160
Butterflies 116

Cabrillo National Monument 137
California Ballet Company 94
California Bicycle Inc. 157
California Center for the Arts 87
California Surf Museum 81
Camping 18, 119, 123, 133
Carlsbad Flower Fields 169
Carlsbad Skate Park 45
Caves 107, 159
Ceramicafe 36
Charmaine and Maurice Kaplan Theatre 99
Children's Discovery Museum of North County 67
Children's Pool 106
Chinese Historical Museum 139
Chollas Lake Park 132
Christian Community Theater 88
Christian Youth Theater 88
Christmas on the Prado 170
Chrysler Jeep Speed Festival 172
Chula Vista Bayside Park 132
Chula Vista Nature Center 108
Cinderella Carriage Company 162
City Ballet of San Diego 93

Classics for Kids 101
Claytime Ceramics 36
Coach USA 161
Color Me Mine 36
Computer Museum of America 81
Contactours & Charter Services 161
Coronado 17
Coronado Historical Museum 18
Coronado Municipal Beach 52
Coronado Playhouse 18
Corporate Helicopters 166
Costume Rentals 37

Del Mar City Beach 53
Dinosaurs 79
Double Decker Bus & Tours 161

Escondido Sports Center 45

Family Christmas Tree Farm 114
Family Fun Centers 53
Family Theater 87
Fern Street Circus 90
Film Festivals 98
Firehouse Museum 141
Fishing 119, 125, 132, 158
Fleet Science Center Space Theater 98
Fleet Week 172
Fossils 71, 79, 81
Free Flight Aviary 110
Free or Almost Free 15, 17, 19, 23, 51, 59, 62, 67, 69, 71, 75, 81, 82, 83, 87, 91, 95, 98, 105, 106, 108, 110, 111, 119, 122, 123, 125, 127, 128, 130, 132, 137, 139, 141, 142, 144, 146, 148, 149, 151, 152, 160, 163, 169, 170, 172, 173, 174, 176, 179

Gaslamp Bicycle and Pedicab Company 157
Gaslamp Quarter 19
Ghosts 23, 150, 160
Golf 16, 17, 62
Gondola Company 159
Grape Day Park-Heritage Walk 151
Grayline San Diego 167
Grove Bowling Center 35
Gyminny Kids 55
Gypsy Treasure Costumes 38

H & M Landing 158
Habitat for Humanity Re-Store 39
Happy Trails Horse Rental 115
Heath Davis House 19
Helen Woodward Animal Center 113
Heritage of the Americas Museum 81
Heritage Park 151
Hiking 16, 17, 19, 27, 105, 119, 121, 124, 126, 128, 129, 131, 132, 133, 137, 148
Hornblower Cruises 158
Horton Square Ice Rink 42

I Made it Myself! 39
Ice Chalet 42
Indoor Gyms 51, 54, 55
Insects 79, 116
Island Tumble 55

JW Tumbles 55

Knorr Candle Shop 39
Knott's Soak City 57

La Jolla Kayak & Co. 159
La Jolla Shores 53, 116
Lake Miramar 132
Lake Poway Park 119

Lakeside Western Days and Rodeo 173
Lamb's Players Theatre 18, 102
Laser Tag 42, 54, 60
Learning Express 34
Legoland 21
Leslie Farms 113
Libraries, Children's 36
Los Penasquitos Canyon Preserve 121

Marie Hitchcock Puppet Theatre 15, 102
Marine Corps Recruit Depot Command Museum 82
Maritime Museum 99, 142
Markets, Public 40, 105
Michaels 39
Military History 18, 81, 126, 138, 148, 165
Mingei International Museum 82
Minigolf 53
Mira Mesa Lanes 35
Miramar Air Show 172
Mission Bay Park 122
Mission Bay Sportcenter 48, 159
Mission Beach Club 157
Mission San Diego de Alcala 144
Mission San Luis Rey de Francia 152
Mission Trails Regional Park 124
Mission Valley River Walk 132
Monarch Butterfly Program 116
Moonlight Beach 53
Mount Woodson Castle 152
Museum of Contemporary Art 82
Museum of Making Music 69
Museum of Man 71

Museum of Photographic Arts 82
Music 15, 69, 87, 96, 101, 128, 171, 176
My Gym 55

Native Americans 71, 81, 126, 128, 145, 146, 148
Navy Base Tour 18

Ocean Beach 116
Ocean Beach Kite Festival 174
Ocean Beach Surf Shop 48
Oceanography 65
Oceanside City Beach 53
Oktoberfest 176
Old Globe Theatre 91
Old Poway Park 146
Old Town 23
Old Town Trolley Tours 161
Original Bike Cab Company 157

Pacific Beach Surf Shop 48
Parkway Bowl 35
Party City 38
Party Supplies 37
Pedicabs 156
Pinery Pumpkin Patches/Tree Farm 114
Places to Paint Pottery 43
Presidio Hills Golf Course 62
Presidio Park 126
Public Transit 160, 163

Quail Botanical Gardens 127
Qualcomm Stadium 62

Recreation Centers 44
Reuben H. Fleet Science Center 73
Rinks, Ice 41
Rinks, Roller 41
Rock Climbing, Indoor 56
Robb Field Skateboard Park 45

Rohr Park 133
Rollerskateland 42

San Diego Aerospace
    Museum 82
San Diego Automotive
    Museum 82
San Diego Ballet 93
San Diego Children's Choir 102
San Diego Civic Youth Ballet
    102
San Diego Coronado Ferry 159
San Diego County Fair 177
San Diego Hall of Champions
    83
San Diego Harbor Excursion
    159
San Diego Historical Society
    Museum 83
San Diego Ice Arena 42
San Diego Junior Theatre 94
San Diego Model Railroad
    Museum 75
San Diego Museum of Art 77
San Diego Natural History
    Museum 79
San Diego Opera 102
San Diego Public Library 36
San Diego Scenic Tours 161
San Diego School of Creative
    and Performing Arts 102
San Diego Symphony 96
San Diego Trolley 163
San Diego Youth Symphony
    102
San Elijo Lagoon 133
San Pasqual Battlefield State
    Park 148
Sandy's Rental Stable 114
Santee Drive-in 99
Seaforth Landing 159
Seaport Village 59
SeaWorld 25
Serra Cooperative Library
    System 36

Shopping 17, 19, 33, 51, 59, 171,
    173
Silver Strand State Beach 53
Skate San Diego 43
Skateboard Parks 45
Skateworld 42
Skating, Ice 18, 42
Skating, In-line 17, 41, 42, 45,
    51, 123, 125, 132, 133, 157
Solid Rock Gym 56
South Bay Drive-in 99
Space 73, 82
Starlight Musical Theatre 100
Stein Farm 152
Stelzer Park 133
Sunset Bowl 35
Surfing 46, 48, 81, 159
Sweetwater Farms 115
Swimming 16, 46, 51, 123
Swimming Pools 16, 46, 51

"Tabletops" at Cardiff 116
Tecolote Canyon 133
Tennis 16, 17, 62
Tidelands Park 17
Tidepools 115
Tijuana River Estuary 129
Timken Museum 83
Torrey Pines State Reserve 130
Trail Rides 114
Trains 16, 75, 105, 137, 146,
    151, 155
Trolley Tours 160

U.S. Open Sandcastle Competi-
    tion 179
Ultrazone 60
U-pick Farms 113

Valley Drive-in 99
Vertical Hold 56
Villa Montezuma 149

Washington Street Skate Park
    45

Waterslides/Water Parks 22, 57
Weidner's Gardens 113
Wild Animal Park 27
Williams Worm Farm 116
Woodglen Vista Skate Pocket
  46
Workshops/Camps/Programs
  22, 26, 28, 30, 34, 39, 42, 43,
  44, 46, 48, 55, 56, 62, 66, 72,
  74, 78, 80, 82, 89, 90, 92, 93,
  95, 97, 102, 109, 112, 115, 119,
  121, 124, 128, 131, 133, 138,
  169, 175

World-famous San Diego Zoo
  29

YMCA Krause Family Skate Park
  46

Zany Brainy 34

THE LOBSTER KIDS' CITY EXPLORERS SERIES

$12.95 US · $17.95 CDN

The Lobster Kids' Guide to Exploring
CHICAGO
By Ed Avis
ISBN 1-894222-40-7

The Lobster Kids' Guide to Exploring
LAS VEGAS
By Heidi Knapp Rinella
ISBN 1-894222-29-6

The Lobster Kids' Guide to Exploring
SAN FRANCISCO
By David Cole and Mary Lee Trees Cole
ISBN 1-894222-28-8

The Lobster Kids' Guide to Exploring
SEATTLE
By Shelley Arenas
and Cheryl Murfin Bond
ISBN 1-894222-27-X

Available in all bookstores
or order from www.lobsterpress.com